# DELEGATE

# Multiply Your Impact

*Written by*
*Frank F. Huppe, Ph.D.*

**National Press Publications**
A Division of Rockhurst College Continuing Education Center, Inc.
6901 West 63rd Street • P.O. Box 2949 • Shawnee Mission, KS 66201-1349
1-800-258-7248 • (913) 432-7757

***DELEGATE Multiply Your Impact***
Published by National Press Publications
© 1992 National Press Publications
A Division of Rockhurst College Continuing Education Center

Printed in the United States of America.

2  3  4  5  6  7  8  9  10

ISBN #1-55852-093-7

# Dedication

*To Dorothy, John, Susan and Michael*

*For their love and understanding through the years*

---

# Acknowledgments

I am grateful to Ellen Walterscheid for skillfully editing the text and offering support throughout the project.

I am especially grateful to Peggy Pennington for her friendship, encouragement and extraordinary effort and help with all phases of manuscript preparation.

**Frank F. Huppe**

# About Rockhurst College Continuing Education Center, Inc.

Rockhurst College Continuing Education Center, Inc., is committed to providing lifelong learning opportunities through the integration of innovative education and training.

National Seminars Group, a division of Rockhurst College Continuing Education Center, Inc., has its finger on the pulse of America's business community. We've trained more than 2 million people in every imaginable occupation to be more productive and advance their careers. Along the way, we've learned a few things. Like what it takes to be successful ... how to build the skills to make it happen ... and how to translate learning into results. Millions of people from thousands of companies around the world turn to National Seminars for training solutions.

**National Press Publications** is our product and publishing division. We offer a complete line of the finest self-study and continuing-learning resources available anywhere. These products present our industry-acclaimed curriculum and training expertise in a concise, action-oriented format you can put to work right away. Packed with real-world strategies and hands-on techniques, these resources are guaranteed to help you meet the career and personal challenges you face every day.

# Legend Symbol Guide

 Checklist to help you identify issues for future application

 Exercise that reinforces your learning experience

 Questions that help you to apply the critical points to your own solutions

 Example to clarify and illustrate important issues

**C A S E   S T U D Y** Real-world case study to help you apply the information you've learned

# *C*ONTENTS

# Contents

# CHAPTER 1

# Delegation — What Is It and Why Do It?

Today, more than ever, managers must learn to use their time effectively. Whether you work in a large corporation or in a small business, how you use your time will determine what impact you have on your company. As a manager, you have many responsibilities, and most days seem to have too few hours for you to do all you must do. If you're to have an impact, you must learn to control your time and not let it control you. And you must recognize that if you try to do everything yourself, the days will *never* have enough hours. That's guaranteed!

You can take better control of your time in many ways. You may arrive at the office much earlier than everyone else (or stay much later) so you can work without interruption. You may prepare a detailed schedule for each day, blocking off certain times for certain activities. You may develop a comprehensive filing system so you can always retrieve the memo you need without wasting time searching for it. You may prioritize your tasks so you can allocate your time to those that are most important. All of these approaches — or some variation of them — will help you control your time better.

But if you want to be a truly effective manager by broadening your impact in your organization and strengthening your chances for advancement, you must learn to delegate.

1

## What Is Delegation?

According to Webster, to delegate is:

- To entrust to another

- To appoint as one's representative

- To assign responsibility or authority

> *" ... Think of delegation as a process with several steps."*

Delegation is also defined as "the act of empowering to act for another." Although these dictionary definitions are helpful, they don't fully suit our purposes. They suggest that delegation is a single act, but it's more useful and accurate to think of delegation as a process with several steps. In this book, we'll examine those steps, and you'll learn how to multiply your productivity by delegating the right things to the right people at the right time.

Since the dictionary definitions fall short, let's use the following working definition:

**Delegation is assigning to others specific tasks and the authority to complete those tasks, with mutually agreed-upon methods for evaluating the completed work.**

You may feel that you already delegate effectively and don't need much additional skill in that area. But how well *do* you delegate? Could improved delegation make your job easier and more interesting? Management experts have devised many quizzes to show managers how they rate as delegators. Use the following checklist to help you rate yourself. Answer each of the questions "yes" or "no."

## How Well Do You Delegate?

\_\_\_\_ 1. Are you a perfectionist? Are you proud of it?

\_\_\_\_ 2. Do you take work home regularly?

\_\_\_\_ 3. Do you work longer hours than your people do?

\_\_\_\_ 4. Do you spend too much time doing for others?

\_\_\_\_ 5. Do you often wish you could spend more time with your family?

\_\_\_\_ 6. When you return to the office, is your "IN" basket too full?

\_\_\_\_ 7. Do you keep a hand in the job you held before your last promotion?

\_\_\_\_ 8. Do people often interrupt you with queries or requests?

\_\_\_\_ 9. Can you immediately name your top three work goals?

\_\_\_\_ 10. Do you spend time on routine details that others could handle?

\_\_\_\_ 11. Do you like to keep a finger in every pie?

\_\_\_\_ 12. Do you rush to meet deadlines?

\_\_\_\_ 13. Are you unable to keep on top of priorities?

\_\_\_\_ 14. Do you frequently feel overworked?

\_\_\_\_ 15. Is it hard for you to accept ideas that others offer?

\_\_\_\_ 16. Do you attract followers rather than leaders?

\_\_\_\_ 17. Do you give overly detailed instructions to your people?

\_\_\_\_ 18. Do you believe higher-level managers should work more?

\_\_\_\_ 19. Do you hold daily staff meetings?

\_\_\_\_ 20. Do you worry that your employees will show you up?

If you answered "yes" to only one or two of the above questions, you are doing well as a delegator. If you answered "yes" to more than three questions, you could improve your delegation skills.

## Why Delegate?

At this point you may ask, "Why is delegation important? Why should I try to improve? What's in it for me?" Those are reasonable questions. Good delegation takes time and effort, so why should you bother?

In his national best-seller, *The Seven Habits of Highly Effective People,* management and leadership authority Stephen R. Covey says that "...effectively delegating to others is perhaps the single most powerful high-leverage activity there is." And time-management consultant Harold L. Taylor states unequivocally: "Delegation is the most important part of being a manager." Those are strong endorsements of the value and importance of delegation, but what *are* the benefits that make it so powerful? Why *is* delegation so essential to the effective manager?

## If Only I Had More Time ...

One of the main benefits of delegation is pretty obvious. It can save time. You have many responsibilities as a manager, and most days seem to have too few hours for you to do all you must do. If you can successfully delegate some of your activities or tasks to others, you can reduce your own time pressures.

Note the word "successfully" in the last sentence. That's important. If you just dump some of your work on someone else without proper planning and preparation, then your attempt to delegate may fail. If it fails, you must deal with a situation that probably will take more of your time to correct than the original task alone would have taken. In that case, you've aggravated your time bind, not improved it. So it's extremely important to plan and prepare properly before you delegate an activity or task to someone else. We'll talk more about proper planning and preparation later.

But first, consider that the higher you climb the managerial ladder, the less time you should spend "doing" specific tasks. Instead you should spend more time *planning.* Successful delegation frees that time and enables you to contribute to your organization in a more significant way. As a manager, you should approach planning for the future as one of your most

4

important functions. But frequently time pressures force planning lower on your priority list. When that happens, both you and the organization suffer.

In general, decisions should be made and tasks performed at the lowest level possible in an organization. This becomes a practical necessity for an organization to run smoothly and efficiently.

For example, if a clerk in stationery supplies can decide what paper clips to order and knows how to place the order, then the clerk should take care of it without involving anyone at a higher level. This frees the clerk's supervisor and manager to devote their efforts to decisions and tasks more appropriate for their positions and responsibilities.

On the other hand, suppose you're the manager of the section that includes stationery supplies and you want to decide yourself what paper clips to order. You did a thorough study on paper clips several years ago, and you're sure no one else in your section knows as much as you do on the subject. If this reflects the way you operate, the results are predictable:

- You'll become overwhelmed and exhausted trying to handle trivial details as well as the things you should be doing.

- Your people will become bored and frustrated.

- Your entire organization will bog down and become paralyzed and ineffective.

No one really benefits from such a situation — except the competition.

If someone who reports to you is perfectly capable of performing a task, then you shouldn't spend your time working on that task. If you do, you waste your time, deny the other person a development opportunity and weaken the entire organization. As a manager, your role is to strengthen your people and build their confidence, not frustrate them. So you must learn to delegate.

*"First and foremost as a manager or supervisor ... your job is to get things done through other people ... You are paid to manage, not perform every task."*

*— Mary Ann Allison and Eric Allison*

## EXERCISE

Take a few minutes to think about your last full day on the job. On this list, write down 10 tasks or activities you engaged in that day. Use just a few words to describe each. Ignore the last two columns for now.

| Item No. | Task or Activity | Must Do Myself | Could Delegate |
|----------|------------------|----------------|----------------|
| 1. | _____ | _____ | _____ |
| 2. | _____ | _____ | _____ |
| 3. | _____ | _____ | _____ |
| 4. | _____ | _____ | _____ |
| 5. | _____ | _____ | _____ |
| 6. | _____ | _____ | _____ |
| 7. | _____ | _____ | _____ |
| 8. | _____ | _____ | _____ |
| 9. | _____ | _____ | _____ |
| 10. | _____ | _____ | _____ |

When you've completed the list, review each item and ask yourself whether it was something that only you could have handled or something that someone in your group could have done. If you're convinced that only you could have shouldered a given task or activity, put a check mark in the "Must Do Myself" column. If someone in your group could have handled it, put a check mark in the "Could Delegate" column.

If most of your check marks are in the "Must Do Myself" column, you may already use some kind of selection process to decide which tasks to do yourself and which ones to delegate to others. (In Chapter 3 you'll learn how to improve your selection process for deciding what should and should not be delegated.)

If most of your check marks are in the "Could Delegate" column, you've already recognized that many things you do could be done by others. The challenge then becomes to determine *why* you're not delegating tasks or activities you acknowledge could be done by others. (In Chapter 2 you'll learn about barriers to delegation.)

It may be obvious to you that delegating tasks to others will free up time you can devote to higher-level activities such as planning, a definite benefit for a manager. However, some of the other advantages of delegation may not be so obvious.

## Developing People

Developing people is — or should be — a fundamental responsibility of every manager. No organization will survive for long if developing people is not a basic belief and practice in the organization. As a manager, you should always look for ways to train and develop your people. And delegation is one of the most powerful and effective ways you have to build your employees' skills.

Delegation gives your employees a chance to learn and grow. Properly done, it will encourage initiative and result in job satisfaction. When you delegate an important task to someone, you demonstrate your confidence in that person. That builds self-esteem.

> *"You (the supervisor) must have an immediate subordinate to whom you can delegate authority. If you don't, train someone."*
>
> *— Homer T. Rosenberger*

If your employees feel you're providing opportunities for them to grow, they are more likely to be motivated and enthused. They will feel that you are genuinely interested in their career growth and not just in your own. They'll make that extra effort to complete the delegated task successfully because they want to satisfy you and themselves.

Many managers unintentionally treat their employees in a way that leads to less-than-optimum performance. They criticize when they should encourage. They reprimand when they should support. They talk when they should listen. Employees who get instructions tinged with doubt or criticism are less likely to believe they can do a good job. The way you treat your people is often influenced by what you expect of them. If your expectations are high, productivity will likely be high. If your expectations are low, productivity will likely be low. An employee's performance tends to rise or fall to meet the manager's expectations. You should keep this in mind, especially when delegating to your people.

For the delegation to be a positive development experience, you must communicate your *high expectations for success*. For example:

- If you ask John to develop a new safety procedure for the shop lathe, suggest how important his effort is to the safety of everyone in the group. Urge him to talk to others for ideas. Tell him you expect his write-up to set the standard for other write-ups in the new safety manual. Make sure he knows that you *expect* him to be successful in developing the new procedure.

- If you ask Susan to take responsibility for organizing the next team meeting, explain to her what topics she needs to include and what you want to accomplish. Encourage her to consider the order of the topics so the meeting flows smoothly. Let her know that you *expect* her efforts will result in a successful, productive team meeting.

- If you ask Michael to design the layout for your new offices, give him information about space requirements and equipment size. Tell him that you were pleased with other layouts he prepared for smaller jobs and that you're confident he can now handle more complex assignments. Tell him you *expect* the new office layout to be a credit to his design capabilities.

> *"A good manager is a man who isn't worried about his own career but rather the careers of those who work for him."*
>
> — *H. M. S. Burns*

> *"The successful man lengthens his stride when he discovers that the signpost has deceived him; the failure looks for a place to sit down."*
>
> —*J. R. Rogers*

In all these cases, your positive attitude, expectations of employees and words of encouragement will not guarantee success, but they will definitely increase the odds for it.

## EXERCISE

In this section, we've focused on developing people as one of the main benefits of delegation. Now consider your own experiences to see how delegation by your boss has influenced your own development.

Think back over the past few months, and identify three instances when a task was delegated to you. If possible, select three *different* kinds of tasks or activities. Then, for each example, complete one of the following worksheets. (If you can't think of three things delegated to you in the last few months, you may need to remind your boss how important delegation is for your development! You may also need to sell yourself, your skills and your knowledge more effectively, and be sure your boss *knows* you're eager to help.)

*"The art of governing consists in not allowing men to grow old in their jobs."*

*— Napoleon Bonaparte*

9

## EXERCISE

### Example #1

**Task/Activity Delegated (brief description):**

_____

_____

_____

_____

**In discussing this task/activity with you, did your boss:**

|  | YES | NO |
|---|---|---|
| • Clearly describe what results were expected? | ___ | ___ |
| • Establish a deadline for completing the task? | ___ | ___ |
| • Grant the authority required for you to act? | ___ | ___ |
| • Make it clear who was responsible for what? | ___ | ___ |
| • Let you decide how to get the results? | ___ | ___ |
| • Provide the needed resources? | ___ | ___ |

During the discussion, did your boss suggest that
the task would help you learn, grow or develop?       ___ ___

As you look back on this particular delegation
experience, do you feel it contributed to your
growth or development?       ___ ___

## EXERCISE (Continued)

### Example #1 (Continued)

If you answered "yes" to the last question, describe below how the experience contributed to your personal development.

If you answered "no," write what you think your boss could have done differently that would have made the experience more worthwhile.

_____

_____

_____

_____

_____

_____

_____

_____

_____

_____

**EXERCISE  (Continued)**

## Example #2

**Task/Activity Delegated (brief description):**

_____

_____

_____

_____

**In discussing this task/activity with you, did your boss:**

|  | YES | NO |
|---|---|---|
| • Clearly describe what results were expected? | ___ | ___ |
| • Establish a deadline for completing the task? | ___ | ___ |
| • Grant the authority required for you to act? | ___ | ___ |
| • Make it clear who was responsible for what? | ___ | ___ |
| • Let you decide how to get the results? | ___ | ___ |
| • Provide the needed resources? | ___ | ___ |

During the discussion, did your boss suggest that
the task would help you learn, grow or develop?          ___ ___

As you look back on this particular delegation
experience, do you feel it contributed to your
growth or development?                                   ___ ___

## EXERCISE (Continued)

### Example #2 (Continued)

If you answered "yes" to the last question, describe below how the experience contributed to your personal development.

If you answered "no," write what you think your boss could have done differently that would have made the experience more worthwhile.

_____

_____

_____

_____

_____

_____

_____

_____

_____

## EXERCISE  (Continued)

### Example #3

Task/Activity Delegated (brief description):

_____

_____

_____

_____

**In discussing this task/activity with you, did your boss:**

|  | YES | NO |
|---|---|---|
| • Clearly describe what results were expected? | ___ | ___ |
| • Establish a deadline for completing the task? | ___ | ___ |
| • Grant the authority required for you to act? | ___ | ___ |
| • Make it clear who was responsible for what? | ___ | ___ |
| • Let you decide how to get the results? | ___ | ___ |
| • Provide the needed resources? | ___ | ___ |

During the discussion, did your boss suggest that
the task would help you learn, grow or develop?        ___ ___

As you look back on this particular delegation
experience, do you feel it contributed to your
growth or development?        ___ ___

## EXERCISE (Continued)

### Example #3 (Continued)

If you answered "yes" to the last question, describe below how the experience contributed to your personal development.

If you answered "no," write what you think your boss could have done differently that would have made the experience more worthwhile.

_____

_____

_____

_____

_____

_____

_____

_____

**EXERCISE  (Continued)**

Now that you've analyzed these three examples, think about how these experiences will influence you the next time *you* delegate. Write down on the following pages any key things you learned that you want to remember to help improve your own delegating.

For example:

- In delegating, it is important to describe clearly what results are expected.

  What will *you* do to be sure your people understand what results are required?

  _____

  _____

  _____

  _____

  _____

  _____

  _____

  _____

## EXERCISE  (Continued)

- When delegating, you should set a deadline for completing the task.

  What will *you* do to be sure no confusion exists about the deadline for the task?

  _____

  _____

  _____

  _____

- Granting the required authority is essential before one can act!

  What steps will *you* take to ensure you grant the necessary authority?

  _____

  _____

  _____

  _____

- A clear statement of who is responsible for what is needed in delegating.

  What will *you* do to guarantee that everyone involved understands who is responsible for what?

  _____

  _____

  _____

  _____

## EXERCISE  (Continued)

• Although you should decide *what* results are required, you should let the delegatee decide *how* to get the results.

What will *you* do to be sure you don't dictate *how* to accomplish the task?

_____

_____

_____

_____

• Without needed resources, no one can accomplish a delegated task.

What will *you* do to ensure that the needed resources are available?

_____

_____

_____

_____

## Benefits to the Organization

The skillful manager can draw on the capabilities of everyone in the organization through delegation. To delegate effectively, you must know your people, their aspirations, their capabilities and their concerns. You must understand their strengths and weaknesses. You must know who is best for which task and who would be wrong for a particular assignment. When you take the time and effort to know your people well and delegate appropriate assignments to them, the number of successful delegation experiences increases.

To learn more about your people:

- Talk to them!
- Review their personnel files.
- Discuss their capabilities with their former bosses.
- Develop a Work Style Profile for each person. (We'll discuss this in Chapter 5.)
- Encourage them to let you know their career goals and aspirations.
- Learn about their families, hobbies and personal interests — *while always respecting their privacy.*

## Other Benefits

We've discussed how delegation:

- Enables managers to save time
- Provides an excellent way to develop people
- Draws on the strengths of the organization

Because no one person has a corner on all the good ideas, delegation can uncover knowledge and talents in your people that you never knew existed. When that happens, it benefits you, the individuals and the whole organization. A can-do attitude spreads through the entire company. The result is an organization with a collective self-confidence that's eager to solve its problems and meet its objectives. Few things a manager can do equal the impact of thoughtful, skillful delegation.

> *"I'm naturally a delegator. I guess I realized early in life that, unless you're going to be a violinist or something, your success will probably depend on other people."*
>
> *— William G. McGowan*

> *"Nothing great was ever achieved without enthusiasm."*
>
> *— Ralph Waldo Emerson*

19

*"That man is great who can use the brains of others to carry out his work."*

*— Donn Piatt*

## Summary

In this first chapter, we've discussed the concept of delegation and described some of its benefits — the *what* and *why* of delegation.

Remember Stephen Covey's remark that "...effectively delegating to others is perhaps the single most powerful high-leverage activity there is"? Think of the implications of that statement. Consider the impact that good delegation practices could have on your own career and organization.

Although the *what* and *why* are important, your real objective is to become proficient in the *how* of delegation. In the following chapters, you'll learn the techniques of successful delegation and *how* to use them in your own job. That's where the payoff is!

## QUESTIONS FOR PERSONAL DEVELOPMENT

1. What is the major emphasis of this chapter?


2. What do you feel are the most important things you learned from this chapter?

    1)

    2)

    3)


3. How can you apply what you learned to your current job?

    1)

    2)

    3)


4. What objectives will you set for improvement? By when (date)?

    | Objective: | By When? |
    | --- | --- |
    | 1) | |
    | 2) | |
    | 3) | |

5. Who can help you most in applying what you learned in this chapter?

6. What are the major roadblocks that might hinder your progress in applying what you learned in this chapter?

**Roadblock:**                                    **Why?**

1)

2)

3)

7. How will you communicate the most important points in this chapter to others in your organization?

8. What preparation is necessary to introduce better delegation?

9. What changes do you expect to make that will better motivate your team?

**Change:**                                    **By When?**

1)

2)

3)

10. How will you monitor your progress to assure that performance has improved or productivity has increased? (reports, meetings, etc.)

11. What work-related problems concern you most in evaluating how you will benefit from this chapter?

12. What changes do you expect to see in yourself one year from now as a result of what you learned in this chapter?

## *C*HAPTER 2

# Barriers to Delegation

Few managers seriously question the benefits of delegation, but many are still reluctant to delegate. You may agree in principle that delegation is a valuable skill that can help you, but in practice you may find reasons or excuses to avoid delegating. In your mind you believe in it, but in your heart you're not so sure.

Because effective delegation is so powerful and can give such a boost to you and your organization, you need to analyze the delegation process to see how it affects your ability to delegate. To improve your skill, you must understand your own situation and find out what prevents you from delegating more effectively. A major step toward improving your delegation skills is to identify barriers that stand in your way. Only by recognizing and understanding those barriers can you learn to overcome them.

In analyzing barriers to delegation, it's important to be honest with yourself. When you delegate a job, you may be uncomfortable. You may feel you're losing control or authority. You may question whether the benefits really justify the risk of letting a task go. If you can understand *why* you're uncomfortable, then you can end or at least reduce your discomfort. That will build your confidence and enable you to strengthen your delegation skills. In this chapter, we'll examine some of those barriers to delegation and help you find ways to overcome them.

> *Only by recognizing and understanding the barriers to delegation can you learn to overcome them.*

Barriers to effective delegation reside in three places:

- You, the manager

- Your employee (the potential delegatee)

- The situation

We'll examine barriers that can arise from each of these sources.

## Barriers in the Manager

Most barriers to delegation dwell in the manager. That's encouraging, because it suggests that you, the manager, can act to remove or overcome them. You don't have to rely on someone else to remove most of the barriers, because you're in control. If the barrier lies within you, then you're the one who can remove it.

One of the first steps to dropping delegation barriers is to *identify the problem.* That may sound obvious, but failure to state the problem clearly is often the main reason no one finds a solution to it. If you take time up front to make sure you understand what the problem is, you're much more likely to solve it and start delegating more effectively.

Earlier we mentioned the importance of being honest with yourself when you analyze barriers to delegation. But *why* is that so important? Honesty is important because your goal is to make yourself a more effective delegator. To do that you must remove the barriers that prevent you from delegating effectively. But before you can remove them, you must identify and understand them — a step that takes honesty.

For example, suppose you're considering asking Sally, one of your most competent employees, to prepare an important group progress report that you've always written in the past. Sally is quite capable, and writing the report would be a good development experience for her. However, you finally decide not to delegate that task to her because she's "too busy." At least, that's what you tell yourself. But are you being honest with yourself?

*"A problem well stated is a problem half-solved."*

*— Charles F. Kettering*

*"This above all: to thine own self be true."*

*— William Shakespeare*

You also know that Sally is excellent at organizing her work and writes very well. If Sally writes the report, your boss may compare her work with your own. He may even decide that her report beats those you have submitted. So Sally becomes — in your mind — a threat to you. Rather than delegate the report-writing to Sally, you do it yourself — because she's "too busy." But if you're honest with yourself, you know that's not the real reason. You know you felt threatened, so you passed up an ideal delegation opportunity.

To remove barriers to delegation, you must first identify and understand the real barriers — a step that demands honesty.

## EXERCISE

In Chapter 1, you made a list of tasks and noted whether you had to do them yourself or could delegate them. Review that list and write below the tasks or activities you said you could delegate but didn't. Then, for each one, write the reason you decided not to delegate that task. Be honest with yourself.

| Task or Activity | Reason |
| --- | --- |
| | |
| | |
| | |
| | |
| | |
| | |
| | |

Let's examine some barriers to delegation frequently found in managers and try to understand them. As we do, consider your own experience and decide whether these barriers have kept you from delegating. Remember, the first step toward overcoming a barrier is to honestly identify and understand it.

## I Can Do It Better

As a manager, you've probably considered delegating a task and then said to yourself: "I can do it better." That's not surprising or unusual. If it's a task you've performed many times and could do with little effort, you probably *could* do it better. But you have to think beyond just completing that one task. You must look at the larger picture and consider the long-term results of your delegating or failing to delegate.

Suppose you've been manager of your section for five years, and for the last four years you've prepared the section's annual budget request. You know the routine, and you can probably do the job better than anyone else. To prepare the request, you must use your organizational skills and must meet and talk extensively with others in the section.

Last year you asked Marilyn, a supervisor reporting to you, to help you prepare the request. You'd been pleased with her performance as a supervisor and wanted to give her some experience with the budget process. She was eager to help and turned out to be a whiz at the computer program you used to develop the budget figures. Although she made one minor error in the material she prepared for you, she understood what caused it as soon as you asked about it and corrected it right away. Overall, she did a very good job. After you submitted the budget request, she even asked you for reading suggestions to learn more about budgeting. From discussions you've had with her, you know she followed through and studied those references. She also talked with other employees in the section to learn their views on the budgeting process.

Now it's budget-preparation time again, and your boss has just asked you to lead a task force to find the cause of failures in a recently released product. He wants that to be your highest priority and says it will take "all your waking hours." You consider asking Marilyn to prepare the budget request, but you find yourself thinking: "I can do it better."

In reviewing the situation, you convince yourself you can handle the task-force assignment *and* prepare the budget request, but it will take 60-hour weeks for more than a month. Now you must decide whether to delegate the budget-preparation task to Marilyn or do it yourself because you "can do it better."

The following questions will help you decide whether to delegate the task to Marilyn:

1. Even though I can do it better, can Marilyn do the job *satisfactorily?*

2. What would happen if I worked on the budget and did not devote enough effort to my task-force assignment?

3. What are the benefits if I delegate the task to Marilyn? For me? For Marilyn? For the organization?

4. What are the risks? For me? For Marilyn? For the organization?

5. How will I handle all my other responsibilities if I'm working on both the budget and the task force?

As a manager, you may frequently encounter the *I can do it better* barrier. If you do, you should take steps to ensure that your people are trained and equipped to handle tasks you delegate. With your support, encouragement and guidance, they'll develop in their jobs. Hopefully, you'll soon be saying: "*They* can do it better." That should be your objective.

## I Lack Confidence in My People

One of the most damaging of managers' barriers to delegation is lack of confidence in their people. When you withhold delegation because you lack confidence in your people, you deny them the opportunity to develop the very abilities they need to build confidence. It's a never-ending cycle. A manager's claims that his people can't handle delegated tasks become self-fulfilling prophecies. If your people can't handle delegation, that may say more about the training environment than about their innate capabilities.

If you feel unable to delegate to your people because you don't trust them, you must take action. Waiting for them to do something to build your confidence is hopeless. You have to demonstrate leadership, take some risk and break the cycle. If you don't, the situation will only deteriorate.

If you're sure you've identified lack of confidence as the issue, then try to understand *why* you don't have confidence in your people. On the following chart, write down the name of each person in your group and force yourself to write beside each name *why* you lack confidence in that person. Be specific. Don't rely on fuzzy generalizations. For example, write "Failed to complete three delegated tasks" rather than "Unreliable." Or "Submitted two financial reports with serious errors" rather than "Careless."

*"He who has no faith in others shall find no faith in them."*

*— Lao-Tzu*

## EXERCISE

| Name | Do I lack confidence? | If so, why? |
|------|----------------------|-------------|
| _____ | _____ | _____ |
| _____ | _____ | _____ |
| _____ | _____ | _____ |
| _____ | _____ | _____ |
| _____ | _____ | _____ |
| _____ | _____ | _____ |
| _____ | _____ | _____ |
| _____ | _____ | _____ |
| _____ | _____ | _____ |
| _____ | _____ | _____ |
| _____ | _____ | _____ |

*"If ... you find specific reasons for your lack of trust ... you've made progress because you now have an issue you can address ... ."*

This process should help you overcome the *lack of confidence* barrier. If you find you can't give explicit reasons for your lack of confidence in a particular person, then you may decide no real reasons exist. Hopefully, this will lead you to reassess the situation and decide that no *lack of confidence* barrier prevents you from delegating tasks to that person.

If, on the other hand, you find specific reasons for your lack of trust in a particular person, you've made progress, because you now have an issue you can address. Instead of dealing with some vague feeling about a person, you can tackle the specific problem you've identified. You can now break the cycle and begin the process to restore or develop confidence in your employee.

Let's consider an example to see what you might do to overcome barriers once you've identified specific reasons for your lack of confidence.

### Example

Every month your plant requires you to submit statistics on the plant's safety performance to the home office. You've always done this job yourself because it involves collecting data on total hours worked, verifying hours lost through injury and using a special formula to calculate the plant safety index for the month. You've considered asking Dennis to collect the data and perform the calculations, but you don't have confidence in his mathematical skills, so you've never delegated the task to him. In this case, there *is* a *lack of confidence* barrier. Nothing is likely to change unless you take action. What can you do?

First, you must determine whether your assessment of Dennis' mathematical ability is true. What is the basis for your belief that he doesn't have the mathematical skills required? Is your belief soundly based, or have you merely assumed Dennis lacked the necessary skills? You should answer that question first. Again, write down *specific incidents* that show Dennis' lack of mathematical ability. If you can't, are you *assuming* without any firm basis that he lacks the ability?

Your investigation may show that Dennis is quite competent in math, contrary to your prior belief. In that case, the reason for your lack of confidence in him vanishes, and the barrier is gone. Hopefully, you'll now delegate the task to him.

But what if your investigation *confirms* your belief that Dennis can't handle math? Then you can congratulate yourself for assessing his skills correctly. You've "justified" your lack of confidence in him, and you can return to doing the monthly safety calculations yourself. Nothing has changed.

However, there's a better alternative — one that is preferable for all concerned. Instead of being satisfied that you were "right" all along, you can act to overcome the barrier.

As manager, you're responsible for creating an environment that encourages and helps your people develop. Providing appropriate training is one aspect of that responsibility. Instead of abandoning Dennis and missing an excellent delegation and development opportunity, you could arrange for someone to help him brush up on his math. You create a win-win situation: Dennis improves his skills, and you develop confidence in him, thereby removing the no-confidence barrier. You can now delegate to Dennis, and the situation improves. You also may delegate, with strong personal supervision, certain tasks that build math skills. Smaller tasks and successes can be great building blocks to improve skill and confidence.

## I Don't Have Time

Managers often feel they don't have time to delegate. That's paradoxical, of course, because one of the primary benefits of good delegation is saving time for the manager. But lack of time remains a very real barrier to delegation for many managers. Why?

To be an effective delegator does take time. You need to spend time planning delegation, meeting with your employee to assign the delegated task and following up as the employee works on the task. You must also devote time to training the people to whom you want to delegate. Since delegation can demand time in all these ways and others, is it any wonder that managers often avoid doing it? Perhaps not.

Let's try to understand this time-barrier paradox so we can find ways to remove it. How can you *save* time if delegation *takes* so much time?

> *"What is done for another is done for oneself."*
>
> — *Latin proverb*

> *"But meantime it is flying, irretrievable time is flying."*
>
> — *Virgil*

**Example**

To understand the paradox, you must consider the impact of the delegation over some reasonable time period. The following example should help clarify what we mean.

**Example**

Suppose you have an assistant, Peggy, who can handle a variety of tasks for you. She routinely deals with confidential matters and is trustworthy and reliable. You've been thinking about asking her to prepare the salary report you must send to division headquarters, but you're sure it would take a full day to teach her what she needs to know. You're very busy and pressed for time. It seems foolish to spend a full day training her when you can prepare the report yourself in half a day. Should you take a day to train her or should you prepare the report yourself?

You really don't know enough to answer that question properly. Important information is missing — information about the time period in question.

If the salary report is submitted only once a year, you may decide it's not worth taking a full day from your busy schedule now to train Peggy, when you could prepare the report yourself in half a day. That's probably a reasonable decision.

On the other hand, if you must submit the salary report monthly, that's a much different situation. If you spend one day training Peggy now, then you'll save yourself almost six days during the next year. That's a good return on the time you invest in training her. Besides, you'll help her learn something new, and that will strengthen her overall ability to contribute. So, you and Peggy *both* benefit. That's a win-win situation.

Of course, other factors could complicate this delegation situation. For example, you may see that you can save substantial time during the next year by training Peggy today, but your calendar is packed with higher-priority tasks, and you really can't take time now to train her. That's a judgment you must make based on all you know about your current and future situation. If you can't train her today, then commit yourself to set aside a day in the near future to spend with her. You can still get a large return on that investment of time.

*"Overcoming the time barrier to delegation is usually straightforward. So often we focus too much on short-term results ... "*

Overcoming the time barrier to delegation is usually straightforward, but it does require you to consider the big picture and weigh the short-term demands on your time against the long-term benefits of delegating. So often we focus too much on short-term results, when a few minutes of analysis will show us the real benefits of taking time to delegate now.

## I'll Lose My CAP (Control, Authority, Power)

Perhaps the most common barrier to delegation in managers is the *CAP* barrier. You struggle with this one when you say to yourself: "I don't want to delegate because I'll lose my *CAP* (control, authority, power)." Many managers find this the most difficult barrier to overcome. They must forsake elements that seem the very essence of being a manager.

When you delegate a job, you attach certain feelings to the transfer of responsibility. You may feel loss of control, authority or power. You may wonder whether you'll get any credit for the completed task. These emotions are common and aren't negative in themselves. However, unless you keep them in check, they can hinder delegation. In extreme cases, if you let them develop into major concerns, they can become destructive and can cripple your performance as a manager. There's no reason to let that happen.

The *CAP* barrier seldom poses a problem for managers with high self-esteem and confidence in their abilities. They realize their value to the organization is not measured by how much control they exercise, how much authority they possess or how much power they wield. Their concept of manager is much broader and focuses on what they can accomplish through their people — not on how much they can control them.

### Case Study

George is a new manager who's ambitious and wants to make a good impression on his boss. He's convinced the harder he works, the more he'll impress her. He puts in long hours and helps his three supervisors with their responsibilities.

> *"Control freaks don't grow good companies."*
>
> *—Jeffery A. Timmons*

**C A S E   S T U D Y**

**C A S E   S T U D Y**

George's boss, Elizabeth, noticed his hard work. He was conscientious and always finished tasks before the deadline. Although he always delivered the required results, Elizabeth thought he seemed tired and irritable.

He was once known for his sense of humor, but that was gone.

A month ago, Elizabeth suggested George try to delegate tasks to his supervisors. She felt he was a promising manager who could contribute more needed planning to the organization, but he seemed too immersed in day-to-day responsibilities. She saw no evidence that George followed her suggestion to delegate, so she decided to talk with him again.

"George, it's been six months since you were promoted to manager, and I just want to see how things are going. Do you think you're adjusting to your new responsibilities?"

"Yes, I feel good about the last six months. I've made a list of all my tasks and activities and blocked out time every week so I'm sure to complete everything. I've made a detailed schedule and can get everything done as long as no unusual requests come up."

"And what do you do when such requests *do* come up?"

"I squeeze them in and do my routine tasks on Saturday."

"Have you tried to delegate any of those 'routine tasks,' George?"

As soon as she said "delegate," George recalled their discussion about that subject a month ago.

"I've thought about it, Elizabeth, but my responsibilities are pretty important. I don't think anyone else can handle them. The supervisors don't have authority to do these jobs, so I need to do them myself. Besides, they don't know *how* to do my jobs."

George thought he'd been persuasive, but he wasn't sure about the look on Elizabeth's face. He'd thought about delegating some tasks, but felt she wouldn't be as impressed with his hard work.

"George, I think you're struggling with some barriers to delegation that you need to overcome. I want to help you identify and understand them."

### Questions

- If you were Elizabeth, what would you say to George?

- How could you help him identify his barriers to delegation?

- What barriers can you identify for George?

- What advice would you give George about delegating some of his "routine tasks"?

- If George finds a way to overcome his barriers to delegation, how would you expect his performance to be affected?

- What dangers do you see if he continues to manage as he has?

- How do you think his three supervisors feel about his failure to delegate?

- What would you suggest to his supervisors?

"... *Even managers are supposed to enjoy their work, so why should they delegate tasks or activities they particularly like?*"

**Example**

## Occupational Hobbies

Some managers enjoy certain aspects of their jobs so much that they refuse to delegate them. These are sometimes called "occupational hobbies." They rationalize that even managers are supposed to enjoy their work, so why should they delegate tasks or activities they particularly like? That's a reasonable question, but let's take a closer look at it.

### Example

Larry is production manager for a small manufacturing company. He oversees personnel and production at three plants. He's hard-working and known for being a good detail person. He's extremely knowledgeable about personal computers and keeps employee records, business financial information, production data and inventory status on his PC. In fact, Larry inputs virtually every bit of data he will ever need on his PC. He loves to work at his computer and sometimes spends three or four hours without a break analyzing all kinds of data on his system.

Larry's assistant, Penny, is also capable on the computer. She has worked with most of the same software packages Larry has and is especially skilled with the spreadsheet program. Although he's well-versed in how his computer operates, Larry is still a two-fingered typist. Penny, on the other hand, learned to type many years ago and is a whiz at the keyboard.

Penny knows about Larry's heavy workload and thinks she may be able to help him with much of it. She knows he uses the spreadsheet program frequently. Since she has special skills with that program, she decides to suggest to Larry that he turn over some of the spreadsheet work to her. In effect, she's taking the initiative to encourage Larry to delegate to her. She sees it as an opportunity to help him and learn more about the business.

Penny has just left Larry's office and is perplexed. She offered to do some of the spreadsheet work for him, giving him several reasons why that would be good for both of them.

Larry was polite and thanked her for her offer, but he flatly refused her suggestion. He said he'd just installed the newest version of the spreadsheet software and wanted to be sure it was working properly. He hinted he didn't think Penny could handle the new version because it was more complex. When she pointed out she'd already been working with it for a month, Larry looked surprised, but he stuck by his decision.

Penny was very disappointed and couldn't understand why Larry hadn't welcomed her suggestion. When she got back to her office, she told her co-worker Ken what had happened. Ken replied that he thought Larry was too devoted to his "occupational hobby" and that it was acting as a barrier to delegation. Penny looked puzzled. "What do you mean, Ken?"

### Questions

- How can you explain to Penny what Ken meant?

- Should Penny have taken the initiative in offering to do some of Larry's spreadsheet work, or should she have waited for him to make the first move? Why?

- What did you detect in Larry's behavior that might suggest he had an "occupational hobby"?

- Larry was hard-working and apparently a successful manager. Can you give him reasons why he should delegate some of his computer activities?

- If Larry were to delegate some spreadsheet work to Penny, what benefits would you expect for him? For Penny? For the organization?

Although no one expects you to delegate away every single task or activity you enjoy, you must discipline yourself to retain only a few. Otherwise, you'll limit your own ability to grow and contribute, and you'll miss many opportunities to develop and strengthen your people. Remember, thoughtful delegation is a win-win proposition.

## Barriers in the Employee

Although most barriers to delegation are found in managers, some reside in their people. As a manager, you can modify your behavior and overcome barriers within you. However, if the barriers lie elsewhere, you must approach the problem differently. The basic approach is still the same:

- Identify the barrier.

- Understand its cause.

- Take action to overcome it.

## Lack of Experience/Competence

No matter how good your intention to delegate, there may be times when your people just can't do the tasks you want to assign them. They may lack the skills and experience required. As a manager who sincerely wants to delegate, you must decide how to overcome this barrier.

One approach is to replace the unskilled or inexperienced workers with those who have the needed skills and experience. Circumstances may require such drastic action, but in most cases other approaches work better.

Recognizing your managerial responsibilities, you can use such situations as opportunities to train your people through delegation. For this to be successful, your people must have the basic capability to learn the new task, and you must have patience. You should never be impatient with your employees for lacking experience if they've never had the opportunity to gain it.

If you decide to use delegation to train your people, you need to create a climate of support and encouragement. Start by delegating relatively simple and routine tasks so your employees can gain confidence through their successes. As their skill and competence increase, you can delegate more difficult or complex assignments. Don't be afraid to stretch your people, but be reasonable. Be sensitive to signs of discouragement or indications you are pushing them too fast. You'll learn more about this in Chapter 6.

It takes patience to use delegation as a form of training, but the results are likely to please you. Once you've trained your people, you can delegate new tasks to them with confidence. As they assume more responsibility, you can devote more time to other activities. Your skillful delegation will spark the entire organization, and its overall capability level will rise.

We'll discuss delegation as a means to develop people in more detail in Chapter 6.

## Avoidance of Responsibility

Another barrier found in employees is avoidance of responsibility. Some workers who are capable, experienced and skillful will frustrate your attempts to delegate to them because they don't want extra responsibility. If you sense that barrier in one of your people, you need to determine *why* he or she avoids additional responsibility. Until you understand the underlying reason, you probably won't overcome the barrier.

Getting to the heart of a person's reasons for avoiding additional responsibility can be difficult because you frequently must deal with his fears and feelings. Your employee may avoid new responsibility for many reasons. Here are four possibilities:

- *Fear of risk.* Accepting responsibility for a delegated task usually involves some degree of risk, and some people fear risk so much they'll avoid it at all costs.

> *"Every human mind is a great slumbering power until awakened by keen desire and by definite resolution to do."*
>
> — *Edgar F. Roberts*

41

- *Fear of punishment for mistakes.* From personal experience or from observation, some people may feel that you won't tolerate mistakes and may in fact frequently punish them. They have no desire to take on new responsibilities in instances where they might make mistakes.

- *Work overload.* Some may feel overworked already and don't want to worsen their situations by assuming more responsibility.

- *No reward expected.* If the organization has never rewarded risk-takers and those who accept additional responsibility, some people see no advantage in increasing their risk or responsibility.

This is another instance when it's important for you, as a manager, to know your people well. If you can develop good rapport with them and build their confidence in you, they're more likely to discuss their reasons for rejecting your delegation attempts. Once you understand their reasons, you can work to convince them it benefits both of you when they accept delegated tasks. Begin by delegating a few easy tasks you're sure they'll complete successfully. Follow up and explain how the task helped you and how it increased their knowledge and capability. With a few successes, they should be more willing to accept additional responsibility in the future.

## EXERCISE

In the first column on the form below, list the names of all
employees who report directly to you. Put a check mark in the
second column if you think a barrier to delegation exists in
that person. If you believe the barrier is either lack of
experience/competence or avoidance of responsibility, put a
check mark in the appropriate column. In the last column, list
the action steps you plan to take to overcome the barrier.

| Name | Barrier? | Experience/ Competence | Avoidance of Responsibility | Action |
|------|----------|------------------------|-----------------------------|--------|
| _____ | ❑ | ❑ | ❑ | _____ |
| _____ | ❑ | ❑ | ❑ | _____ |
| _____ | ❑ | ❑ | ❑ | _____ |
| _____ | ❑ | ❑ | ❑ | _____ |
| _____ | ❑ | ❑ | ❑ | _____ |
| _____ | ❑ | ❑ | ❑ | _____ |
| _____ | ❑ | ❑ | ❑ | _____ |
| _____ | ❑ | ❑ | ❑ | _____ |

## Barriers in the Situation

In some cases, barriers to delegation exist neither in the manager nor in the employee, but they are clearly present and prevent successful delegation. In those cases, the barriers usually lie in the situation.

For example, a barrier associated with staffing problems frequently arises in organizations that are reducing employees. The total workload may remain relatively constant, but it's spread over fewer people. The remaining people feel overloaded. Even though they normally accept delegation and possess the necessary skills to handle it, the situation has created a barrier because they're overworked.

Such a situation presents a real challenge for you. If the organization is consciously trying to reduce employees, you probably can't hire additional people to relieve the workload pressure. You may be able to hire temporary help, but often the organization discourages that. So what can you do?

If there's no way you can add people, it's time to review your current employees again. Are they using their time efficiently? Are they working on tasks that really have to be done? (We'll discuss this more in Chapter 3.) Are they delegating to *their* people? You may need to help them reassess their priorities so that less important — and maybe unnecessary — chores are dropped to the bottom of the list.

It's easy to do things routinely. Downsizing should be a first alert to assess how all time is being spent and to redefine priorities. Hopefully, this will free some time for the tasks you want to delegate. If not, delegate anyway. You may be surprised how well your people respond, show their flexibility and adjust their priorities to accommodate your requests.

You'll sometimes find a situational barrier to delegation in organizations that move from a hierarchical to a matrix structure. In a typical hierarchical structure, you report to only one person. The path for delegation is clear. Your boss delegates to you, and you delegate to those who report to you. However, in a matrix organization, you may have several bosses, or at least it seems that way. Different people may direct you in different aspects of your job. If responsibilities are

*"How can you be in two places at once when you're not anywhere at all?"*

*— The Firesign Theatre*

poorly defined and those people don't communicate well with you or each other, confusion reigns. In this environment you may be reluctant to accept delegation, even though you're usually eager to. Matrix organizations can be very effective, but if lines of authority and responsibility are unclear, the climate for delegation suffers. The situation itself becomes the barrier to delegation.

You may also find situational barriers to delegation in organizations with unclear goals. Delegation is most effective when you can relate delegated tasks to your organizational goals. If you want your efforts to align with goals — and you don't know what the goals are — you'll probably be reluctant to accept delegated tasks. And you *should* be. Why increase your workload with activities that may not further your organization's goals? An organization *needs* clearly stated goals. Without them, the climate discourages delegation. Again, the situation becomes the barrier to delegation.

> *"It is not who is right, but what is right, that is of importance."*
>
> — *Thomas Huxley*

## EXERCISE

Think about your own attempts to delegate during the last month. Did you encounter any barriers that did not seem to be within yourself or within your employees? Would you call them "barriers in the situation"? Describe such a barrier and how you tried to overcome it. Were you successful?

_____

_____

_____

_____

_____

_____

45

## Summary

In this chapter we've explored the three areas in which barriers to delegation fall:

- You, the manager
- Your employees, the potential delegatees
- The situation

Specifically, the barriers for managers tend to include: the belief that they can do the task better; a lack of confidence in their people; a lack—or perceived lack—of time; the belief that they will lose their control, authority and power; or the task has become an occupational hobby.

Barriers in the employee tend to center on either a lack of experience or competence, or avoidance of responsibility.

Sometimes the situation is the barrier—staffing problems, hierarchy or unclear corporate or organizational goals.

One, some or all of these barriers may stand in the way of successful delegation. But identifying them is the first step to overcoming them. In Chapter 3 we will focus on identifying which tasks should, or should not, be delegated.

## QUESTIONS FOR PERSONAL DEVELOPMENT

1. What is the major emphasis of this chapter?


2. What do you feel are the most important things you learned from this chapter?

    1)


    2)


    3)

3. How can you apply what you learned to your current job?

   1)

   2)

   3)

4. What objectives will you set for improvement? By when (date)?

   **Objective:**                    **By When?**

   1)

   2)

   3)

5. Who can help you most in applying what you learned in this chapter?

6. What are the major roadblocks that might hinder your progress in applying what you learned in this chapter?

   **Roadblock:**              **Why?**

   1)

   2)

   3)

7. How will you communicate the most important points in this chapter to others in your organization?

8. What preparation is necessary to introduce better delegation?

9. What changes do you expect to make that will better motivate your team?

| Change: | By when? |
|---------|----------|
| 1) | |
| 2) | |
| 3) | |

10. How will you monitor your progress to assure that performance has improved or productivity has increased? (reports, meetings, etc.)

11. What work-related problems concern you most in evaluating how you will benefit from this chapter?

12. What changes do you expect to see in yourself one year from now as a result of what you learned in this chapter?

# *C*HAPTER 3

# What and What Not to Delegate

You should now have a good understanding of some aspects of delegation and know how to overcome barriers that keep you from delegating effectively. Knowing what the common barriers are lets you be prepared and guard against them. Develop a mind-set that says, "I'll delegate as much as possible. I won't let barriers defeat me." Convincing yourself that you want to delegate whenever possible is half the battle.

## Analyzing Your Job

In this chapter you'll learn how to decide which tasks to delegate and which ones to do yourself. Since tasks for delegation spring from your job responsibilities, you need to make a detailed list of all your tasks and activities. The key word is "detailed." The following Job Activity Analysis form will help you analyze your job.

In the first column, write down every task or activity you perform in your job during a one-month period. Include everything you can think of. For reminders, refer to your calendar, check with your peers, glance at your files and review the stacks on your desk. You want the list to be as complete as possible. (Remember, the list is for your use only, so be honest. If you spend time every day working crossword puzzles, write it down.)

> *"The unexamined life is not worth living."*
>
> *— Socrates*

After you complete the first column, go to the second column and record your estimate of the amount of time you spend *each month* on each task or activity. For some tasks you may find it difficult to estimate the time, but do your best.

Completing the third column is really what this chapter addresses — how do you decide *what* to delegate? However, try to complete the third column now based on your current beliefs about delegating. We'll revisit the Job Activity Analysis form later in this chapter to see whether you've changed your opinion about delegating some tasks. For now, just write "yes" or "no" in the third column for each task based on your initial reaction to the question: "Can I delegate it?" Don't worry about a carefully reasoned response.

Use the fourth column to record any thoughts that occur to you as you review the list. For example, note any tasks you perform that you feel contribute little or nothing to furthering the goals of your organization. You should consider eliminating those, not delegating them. If you write a weekly report that serves no purpose, eliminate it. Don't waste your time on it and don't ask anyone else to waste time on it. More about this later in the chapter.

## EXERCISE

### JOB ACTIVITY ANALYSIS

| Task/Activity | Time Spent Monthly | Can I Delegate It? | Remarks |
|---|---|---|---|
| *Example:* *Inventory darkroom supplies* | *30 min.* | *Yes* | *Give supply list to Matt; recommend stock level to always have on hand* |
| 1. | | | |
| 2. | | | |
| 3. | | | |
| 4. | | | |
| 5. | | | |
| 6. | | | |
| 7. | | | |

**EXERCISE  (Continued)**

## JOB ACTIVITY ANALYSIS (Continued)

| Task/Activity | Time Spent Monthly | Can I Delegate It? | Remarks |
|---|---|---|---|
| 8. | | | |
| 9. | | | |
| 10. | | | |
| 11. | | | |
| 12. | | | |
| 13. | | | |
| 14. | | | |
| 15. | | | |

As you review the list you've made, note those tasks you feel you must handle yourself. Then, after completing this chapter, look at them again to see whether you still feel that way.

After you mark the tasks to eliminate and the ones you must do yourself, consider the rest as candidates for possible delegation. But how do you decide which ones to delegate?

## What to Delegate

Few hard and fast rules exist for deciding which tasks to delegate, because circumstances for individual managers can differ greatly. However, the following guidelines and examples should help you decide as you analyze your own situation:

1. **Delegate the routine and the necessary.** These are the jobs you've done over and over. These are the "necessary" tasks your company routinely dictates. You know them. You know the problems, the peculiarities, the specifics of how to do these jobs. They are also the easiest jobs to delegate. Because you know them so well, you can easily explain and delegate them away.

   Are you required to attend regularly scheduled "informational meetings" that your people could easily handle?

   For the past several years, a local bank vice president was required to attend a monthly council luncheon of all financial institutions in the community. These luncheons primarily served a social function and rarely yielded anything that could not have been handled by the vice president's assistant. The vice president realized that this was a "doing" job, not a "planning" job. He called in the assistant vice president of the bank and explained the function of the luncheon meeting. The young assistant was eager and enthusiastic for a chance to meet his colleagues in a professional setting. It was the perfect opportunity for successful delegation.

> *"There is nothing so hard, but habit makes it easy to us."*
>
> *— Seneca*

2. **Delegate the specialties.** Would you perform surgery on your family? Probably not, unless you happen to be a surgeon. Would you represent yourself in court? Probably not, unless you happen to be a lawyer. You'd look for the most skilled person in the field. The same is true in the office. Take advantage of any specialties that exist in your office. If you're responsible for choosing a new word-processing system, you could do the research yourself or you could delegate the initial research to the computer programmer in your office. If you have a math whiz in the office, that person could assume the responsibility of double-checking the math in all the reports.

   Beware of the "Superman Syndrome." Realize that occasions arise that require you to delegate your normal tasks to skilled professionals such as lawyers, accountants, tax preparers and temporary "overload" employees. Match your need to the skills of the people available to you. Take advantage of their abilities and devote your time to other matters.

3. **Delegate "occupational hobbies."** We discussed these earlier. These are the duties you should have delegated a long time ago, but haven't because they're too much fun. It's OK to keep a couple, but at least recognize them for what they are: easy and enjoyable and much better done by someone else. It may seem paradoxical to delegate the very aspects of your job that you enjoy most. Yet these are often the tasks you hang on to even though they don't represent the best use of your time and energy. They often relate to your area of expertise or earlier positions that you've held in the company.

   A sales manager has been attending the same trade show in Chicago each year for several years. She looks upon the assignment as a chance to get away and see old friends. Actually, it's no longer necessary for the sales manager to be there. One of her sales representatives could achieve the same results. Do you see yourself in this or comparable situations? Are you simply indulging yourself? Wouldn't your career be better served by spending the time in other ways? Take a look at your priorities.

4. **Delegate development opportunities.** One of your primary responsibilities as manager is to develop your people. Delegation of the right task to the right person is an excellent way to do that. You know the responsibilities of your job, and you know the value of certain tasks in helping your people develop. By selective delegation, you can target particular individuals with opportunities to grow.

A research manager was required to give a 15-minute monthly report on a current project in his section. He'd done this every month for two years. It gave him a chance to meet with the research directors, so he enjoyed his monthly time in the spotlight. However, he realized that the directors asked only that a report be given, not that *he* give it. He also recognized that some people in his section would benefit from the experience. When he asked his people about the possibility of making the presentations, he found several who were eager to talk about their projects.

As an experiment for the next three months, his employees presented the monthly reports. The manager was delighted with the results. The research directors complimented him for the fine job his employees did. They also told him how pleased they were that he'd taken the initiative to delegate the presentations to them. The employees appreciated the opportunity and showed surprising improvement in their presentation skills. Everyone benefited because the manager recognized an opportunity to use delegation to develop his people and followed through on it.

*"By selective delegation, you can target particular individuals with opportunities to grow."*

## Eliminating Unnecessary Tasks

It's important to eliminate tasks that do nothing to further the goals of your organization. These unnecessary tasks can soak up a lot of your valuable time. Today, more than ever, you must learn to use your time effectively. Competition in the marketplace is keen. Many organizations are downsizing. Workers are putting in long hours to remain competitive. People are working so hard they have fewer hours to devote to family and leisure activities. Managers are being stretched and often have less help to handle more responsibilities. Rather than adding more hours to your workweek, you must find ways to be more efficient and accomplish more worthwhile tasks in less time. So what can you do?

Evidence suggests that most companies spend significant effort on tasks that should not be done at all! People work hard, but devote too much of their time to activities that don't contribute to the bottom line. They waste time, and time is money.

The problem exists in every organization to some degree. It's found in the executive suite and on the factory floor. Since the poor use of time is so widespread, the organizations that tackle it head-on and find solutions can gain a competitive edge. The basic solution is straightforward:

1. **Identify the tasks/activities in your organization that do not contribute to its goals and objectives.**

2. **Eliminate them.**

It seems so simple, yet it's so powerful. In fact, it's so simple it's often overlooked. This methodical two-step approach can significantly streamline your organization. Look for tasks and activities in your organization that don't contribute to your goals and objectives. Eliminate them. You'll be surprised at how much time is saved — time that you and your company can now spend on productive activities. This is one of the most effective ways to reduce costs by eliminating nonproductive tasks.

You should learn to use this method and apply it regularly in your work environment so that it becomes automatic for you. Use it when reviewing your own activities and encourage your co-workers to use it too.

*"Nothing is more terrible than activity without insight."*

*— Thomas Carlyle*

Sometimes we focus on the wrong objective when we try to streamline time uses. For example, you may identify a task that doesn't seem especially important to meet company goals, but your first reaction is, "How can I do it more efficiently?" or "How can I reduce the number of people performing that task from eight to four?" You may feel you're making progress when you reduce the number of people working on an unneeded task, but you haven't gone far enough. Eliminate these activities, and you'll make a significant contribution to the bottom line.

The following case study illustrates the importance of eliminating unnecessary tasks.

### Case Study

Martha, the new division director, was determined to improve communication in her division and especially between her division and other parts of the company. She decided to issue a comprehensive quarterly report to all managers throughout the company summarizing the status of every project in her division. Each research person was to submit a one-page status report on each of his or her projects every three months. These would be typed and organized alphabetically by the group secretaries. They would send their sections of the report to Mary Anne, Martha's secretary, who would combine all the input, reorganize it, index it and send it out for printing. The report would then be mailed out with a cover letter from Martha.

This procedure was followed for a year, and four issues of the summary report were sent to 150 managers throughout the company. At one of Martha's staff meetings, the agenda included preparation of the fifth issue. During the discussion, Robert, one of Martha's managers, asked her what kind of response she'd gotten from the quarterly reports. Martha hesitated and then admitted she'd received comments from only three recipients of the report, so she wasn't really sure what the reaction had been.

**C A S E  S T U D Y**

57

The meeting participants decided that, instead of the fifth issue, a questionnaire would be sent to all 150 managers to assess how useful the report was to them. When the replies were received, Martha would decide whether to continue the quarterly report.

The questionnaire was prepared and mailed to all the report recipients. More than 80 percent of them returned it within two weeks — an excellent response. Of those responding, only four percent said they found the quarterly report useful and helpful.

Martha decided to discontinue the report.

### Questions

- If you were Martha, what would you have done differently?

- What new tasks and activities can you identify that had to be performed every three months to issue the reports? Were they necessary?

- What could have been done before the *first* issue that might have prevented so much wasted effort?

- What lessons have you learned that you can apply in your own workplace?

## Tasks to Eliminate

No one welcomes economic recessions, but they often provide the incentive for companies to examine their operations more closely to figure out what activities can be modified or eliminated. That's one benefit of recessions. Unfortunately, when the economy turns around, organizations often restore

*"We cannot advance without new experiments in living, but no wise man tries every day what he has proved wrong the day before."*

*—James Truslow Adams*

activities they've eliminated, even if those activities serve no useful purpose. Try to avoid that in your own environment. Be the watchdog who questions the necessity of every task or activity. By doing so, you'll help your organization be more competitive.

The following questions will help you decide whether a task or activity should be eliminated:

- Who are the recipients of this report, service, task, etc., and how does it help them?

- Do they truly value it?

- How do we know?

- Does our effort duplicate something another group is doing?

- What would be the consequences if we eliminated it?

- Has anyone determined recently whether this report, service, task, etc. is really needed?

- What is the cost of providing it?

*"Before you worry about whether or not to delegate a task, you should determine whether that task is worth anyone's time and effort."*

- Is the benefit worth the cost?

- How does it contribute to our organization's goals and objectives?

Why are we spending so much time discussing how to eliminate unnecessary tasks when we're supposed to learn about what tasks to delegate? The answer is simple. Before you worry about whether or not to delegate a task, you should determine whether that task is worth *anyone's* time and effort.

### Never delegate an activity or task that should be eliminated!

Armed with the questions you've just read, review the list of activities on your own Job Activity Analysis. For each item, decide whether it should be eliminated. Be honest with yourself. If you have doubts about a particular item, discuss it with your boss or co-workers. Clearly mark those tasks or activities you feel should be eliminated.

If you can eliminate an unnecessary task yourself, do it. If it's something your boss has asked you to do, you may need to take a different approach. Explain to the boss that you've analyzed the task and determined it can be eliminated. Give your reasons. (An approach that almost always works is to explain that the cost of your spending time on a particular task or activity isn't justified by the benefit of it. Bosses like to save money.)

Tossing out items on your list of responsibilities and admitting that you're wasting time on things that don't need to be done may make you nervous. After all, if you toss out too many, you may eliminate the reason for your position! What would your boss say if you told him or her that you analyzed your job and found that half the things you do don't really contribute to the company's objectives?

If your boss is any good at all, he or she will commend you for what you've done. Every manager should do what you've done. In fact, all managers should try to work themselves out of a job. You should constantly look for tasks and activities that don't contribute to the organization's objectives or to the bottom line, then eliminate them.

Encourage your employees to identify unnecessary tasks too. When they do, publicize their efforts. Put their pictures on the bulletin board. Feature them in the company newspaper. Acknowledge them at special meetings. You may also devise some award to recognize their contributions. Give them a medal or plaque. If eliminating a task results in substantial cost savings, you may want to grant a monetary award. Challenge everyone to work for awards. An entire organization examining its activities and trying to eliminate unnecessary tasks can have an amazing impact. People really want to do what is important and necessary. Most don't want to waste time on their jobs. And a job that's not worth doing is rarely delegated well!

## What Not to Delegate

Although most managers err on the side of not delegating enough, there's the occasional manager who delegates entirely too much. Certain tasks simply can't be delegated to your people.

Here are guidelines to determine what should not be delegated:

1. **Don't delegate personnel/confidential matters.**
   Personnel decisions (evaluation, promotion or dismissal) are generally touchy and often difficult decisions to make. While you may need the confidential input of your people on personnel issues, the job and responsibility are yours.

   Analyzing your department's job classification and pay scales may seem time-consuming and a prime job for delegation. But it's a job for management because of the personal nature of the task. It's not a job to delegate.

> *"There is nothing so useless as doing efficiently that which should not be done at all."*
>
> *Peter Drucker, management expert*

2. **Don't delegate policy-making.** You can delegate responsibilities and tasks within a certain policy area, but you should never delegate the actual formulation of a policy. Policy sets the limits of decision-making.

   Responsibility for policy-making within specified, limited guidelines may be delegated. Credit managers develop general credit policies of businesses, yet salespeople are often allowed the ability to grant credit to specific customers up to certain dollar limits.

3. **Don't delegate crises.** Crises will inevitably happen. When one does occur, the manager must shoulder the problem and find the solution. That's not the time for you to delegate. When the heat is on, make sure you're there to take the lead.

4. **Don't delegate development of those who report directly to you.** As a manager, one of your primary responsibilities is to develop the people who report to you. More correctly, your responsibility is to create a climate that encourages your people while working with you to develop themselves. Your people should look to you for help with their growth and development. They rely on your experience, your judgment and your knowledge of the organization and its needs to identify activities that will help them grow. This is not a responsibility you should delegate. You may get help from others, but the responsibility belongs to you.

5. **Don't delegate assignments your boss asked you to complete personally.** Your boss may have a special reason for asking you to handle the assignment yourself. If you feel strongly that the assignment is appropriate to delegate to one of your people, discuss it with your boss. Be sure you understand whether you were asked *to do it* or *to get it done*. A misunderstanding could strain the relationship between you and your boss, so you must clarify the request.

Remember that these suggestions for what and what not to delegate are guidelines, not laws etched in stone. They should help you decide whether to delegate a task, but you must make your decision based on what you know about your own situation. Individual or special circumstances may make you do a task the guidelines recommend that you delegate. For example, you may have a routine task that's ideal for delegation, but it *must* be completed tomorrow. You don't have time to train anyone, so you do it yourself. You're the best judge of your situation. You must weigh the pros and cons of delegating a particular task or activity and then decide.

Don't be over-cautious. If the pros and cons of delegating a task seem about even, go ahead and delegate. Monitor the situation. If you become concerned, increase your level of involvement. But don't stop delegating. Your skill will increase with experience, so always look for opportunities to delegate. Don't let barriers stop you.

*"Progress comes from the intelligent use of experience."*

*— Elbert Hubbard*

## EXERCISE

### Review of Job Activity Analysis

Now that you know which tasks or activities to delegate and which ones to keep, take another look at your Job Activity Analysis on page 51. Review each item and note your original answer in the left column headed "Can I Delegate It?" Have you changed your mind about any of your answers? If so, write down the tasks you've changed your mind about and give your reason below.

## Job Activity Analysis
## Revised Delegation Decisions

| Task/Activity | Can I Delegate It? Original Revised | | Reason |
|---|---|---|---|
| _____ | _____ | _____ | _____ |
| _____ | _____ | _____ | _____ |
| _____ | _____ | _____ | _____ |
| _____ | _____ | _____ | _____ |
| _____ | _____ | _____ | _____ |
| _____ | _____ | _____ | _____ |
| _____ | _____ | _____ | _____ |
| _____ | _____ | _____ | _____ |
| _____ | _____ | _____ | _____ |
| _____ | _____ | _____ | _____ |
| _____ | _____ | _____ | _____ |
| _____ | _____ | _____ | _____ |

## Summary

In this chapter you learned the guidelines to help you decide what and what not to delegate. You also learned one of the most effective two-step approaches to streamlining your organization:

1.  Identify the tasks/activities that don't contribute to your organization's goals and objectives.

2.  Eliminate them.

The guidelines showed that, in most cases, you can decide whether to delegate a task based on the nature of the task itself. However, remember to consider the circumstances surrounding a task for potential delegation.

In actual situations, you can't ignore the question of whom the delegatee might be when deciding whether to delegate a particular task. You must consider both the task and the potential delegatee when making your decision. In Chapter 5 we'll see how characteristics of the delegatee can influence your decision.

> *"It ain't what a man don't know that makes him a fool, but what he does know that ain't so."*
>
> *—Josh Billings*

## QUESTIONS FOR PERSONAL DEVELOPMENT

1.  What is the major emphasis of this chapter?


2.  What do you feel are the most important things you learned from this chapter?

    1)


    2)


    3)


3.  How can you apply what you learned to your current job?

    1)


    2)


    3)


4.  What objectives will you set for improvement? By when (date)?

    **Objective:**                          **By When?**

    1)


    2)


    3)

5. Who can help you most in applying what you learned in this chapter?

6. What are the major roadblocks that might hinder your progress in applying what you learned in this chapter?

   **Roadblock:**                     **Why?**

   1)

   2)

   3)

7. How will you communicate the most important points in this chapter to others in your organization?

8. What preparation is necessary to introduce better delegation?

9. What changes do you expect to make that will better motivate your team?

   **Change:**                     **By When?**

   1)

   2)

   3)

10. How will you monitor your progress to assure that performance has improved or productivity has increased? (reports, meetings, etc.)

11. What work-related problems concern you most in evaluating how you will benefit from this chapter?

12. What changes do you expect to see in yourself one year from now as a result of what you learned in this chapter?

# $C$HAPTER 4

# Setting Goals in Delegation

Stated simply, a goal is what you plan to achieve. Confusion about goals is one of the primary causes of problems in organizations. When goals are fuzzy and poorly understood, people can't synchronize their activities with the objectives of the organization. Without alignment, people often work at cross-purposes. The effectiveness of the entire organization suffers.

As a manager, you must be sensitive to setting clear goals for your employees and ensuring they understand them. This applies to all facets of their jobs, not just goals associated with delegation. You can avoid much wasted effort by taking time up front to make sure you and your employees have the *same* understanding about their goals. Fifteen or 20 minutes of thorough discussion and clarification at the start may save weeks of misguided effort in the future.

Don't confuse the concept of being exact in setting goals with the notion of letting employees decide how to achieve them. Be clear in stating *what* is required, but let your people decide *how* to accomplish it.

*"A goal is what you plan to achieve."*

## Characteristics of Goals

The common injunction "Do your best" does virtually nothing to motivate people. If you think about it, that's not surprising. Ambiguity is the opposite of productivity. What does "Do your best" mean? To the worker faced daily with countless priorities and demands, it can mean dozens of things. Because the worker hears it all the time, it comes to mean nothing at all.

*Goals must be specific, clearly stated and clearly measurable.* Goals with these characteristics provide feedback, accountability and evaluation. Well-stated, measurable objectives work miracles to motivate people and improve their performance. If an employee doesn't have a clear idea of the task at hand and doesn't receive feedback after performing it, you can't realistically hold him or her accountable for the task. Help your employee understand the relationship between the delegated task and your organization's goals. Give feedback as he progresses with the task. Unfortunately, the chaotic workplace, where many don't know what to do and seldom get feedback, is the rule rather than the exception in American business.

For goals to be any good, they must be measurable. Build tests into each goal to measure its progress. You should also remember that people understand and respond best when they can measure their own progress, even *without* your feedback. If you ask them to "increase sales by 10 percent," they can tell how well they're doing as they work toward the goal. But if you suggest they "do better next month," they have no idea what you mean and no way to measure progress.

Sound goals should contain three identifiable elements:

1.   An action verb (to increase, to contact, to sell, to enroll, etc.)

2.   A measurable result (five, 50 percent, 3,000, etc.)

3.   A deadline (3 p.m. on June 16)

*"Perfection of means and confusion of goals seem, in my opinion, to characterize our age."*

*— Albert Einstein*

When setting goals and choosing tasks for a "marginal" employee, aim for just a little more work than the employee has been doing. Aim for a target he can reach. You want to build confidence through successful completion of the task. As your employee develops more confidence, he will be able to perform at a higher level. Success builds on success. If you want a successful performer to do more, don't be afraid to aim high.

A time element is crucial to commitments. Ask and agree upon a time for completion. Don't say, "I want you to get your work done soon." Instead say, "The goal is to increase production 10 percent by June 16th." And whatever you do, avoid saying, "Why don't we get together sometime soon and discuss this again?" Rather say, "Let's get together on March 3rd at 3 p.m. for a review of our progress." Establish with your employee the understanding that commitments can be renegotiated, but if they are, you still expect your employee's full commitment to the new terms. Getting a firm commitment takes time on your part, but it's an essential element of good supervision.

Without a commitment to success, the best laid goals are often doomed to fail. Where there's no commitment there's low priority, and low-priority goals are seldom achieved. Therefore, it's crucial to get your employees committed to the goals. Too often we take commitment for granted and overlook this simple step. You want more than nodded approval or tacit acceptance. Go for an outright statement that the person agrees on the goals and the deadlines. For example, you might ask your employee to write down the agreed-upon goals and indicate acceptance by signing his or her name below the goals. Be prepared to include employee suggestions or modifications in your goals and deadlines. Be flexible.

Even when a plan seems workable, you might want to get a written commitment. Many management experts suggest that each goal and the way it will be evaluated should be written on paper. Each goal and its method of evaluation should take no more than 25 words. Put the accountability where it belongs. Train yourself and your people to review these written goals on a regular basis.

> *"It is easier to do a job right than to explain why you didn't."*
>
> *— Martin van Buren*

## EXERCISE

Using the three identifiable elements of sound goals —
action verb, measurable result and deadline — write five
clear goals for your people to achieve. Also indicate how
you would evaluate each goal.

1.   **Goal:**   _____

     _____

     **Method of Evaluation:** _____

     _____

2.   **Goal:**   _____

     _____

     **Method of Evaluation:** _____

     _____

3.   **Goal:**   _____

     _____

     **Method of Evaluation:** _____

     _____

4.   **Goal:**   _____

     _____

     **Method of Evaluation:** _____

     _____

5.   **Goal:**   _____

     _____

     **Method of Evaluation:** _____

     _____

## Common Errors in Goal-Setting

In his book, *Think Like a Manager,* Roger Fritz gives a list of the 20 most common errors in goal-setting. Try to avoid these errors when you set goals with your people:

1. Not clarifying common objectives for the whole unit

2. Setting goals too low to challenge the employee

3. Not using prior results as a basis to find new and unusual goal combinations

4. Not blending the unit's common objectives with those of the larger unit to which it belongs

5. Overloading individuals with inappropriate or impossible goals

6. Not clustering responsibilities in the most appropriate positions

7. Letting two or more individuals believe they are responsible for doing exactly the same things

8. Stressing methods (how) rather than clarifying individual areas of responsibility

9. Putting the emphasis on pleasing the boss rather than achieving the job objective (what)

10. Not having policies as action guides — boss waits for results, then issues *ad hoc* judgments in correction

11. Not probing to discover what employee's program for goal achievement will be. Accepting each goal uncritically without a plan for successful achievement

12. Not adding the manager's (or higher management's) known needs to the program of employees

> *"Don't set goals that are too low to challenge the employee."*

13. Ignoring real obstacles that will face the employee, including emergency or routine duties that consume time

14. Ignoring proposed new goals or ideas for employees and imposing only those the manager wants

15. Not thinking through and acting upon what the manager must do to help the employee succeed

16. Not setting intermediate target dates (milestones) by which to measure the employee's progress

17. Not having new ideas introduced from outside the organization, thereby freezing the status quo

18. Failing to permit new goals in place of stated objectives that are less important

19. Failing to discard previously agreed-upon goals that have subsequently proven unfeasible, irrelevant or impossible

20. Not reinforcing successful behavior when goals are achieved

*Discard previously agreed-upon goals that have subsequently proven unfeasible, irrelevant or impossible.*

## EXERCISE

You can convert this list of errors in goal-setting into a "to do" checklist by rewording each item into a positive action statement. The first three have been done for you as examples. Complete the rest of the list by rewording each common error into an action statement.

1. *Set and clarify common objectives for the whole unit.*

2. *Set goals high enough to challenge the employee.*

3. *Use prior results to find new and unusual goal combinations.*

4.

5.

6.

7.

8.

9.

10.

11.

12.

13.

14.

15.

16.

17.

18.

19.

20.

> *"Management by objectives works if you know the objectives. Ninety percent of the time you don't."*
>
> *— Peter Drucker*

**C
A
S
E

S
T
U
D
Y**

Use the checklist you just created when you prepare to delegate. Goal-setting with your employees leads to success. It will help you set goals that are clear, realistic and aligned with your organization's objectives. Setting goals is the first step toward achieving them.

**Case Study**

After wide experience elsewhere, Beverly joined a large pharmaceutical company. She's capable, outgoing and anxious to contribute. She knows she's now in a new organization with new objectives. She's eager to learn her new goals so she can contribute. She works hard, but she knows hard work on the wrong goals isn't productive — and she wants to be productive.

After a month in her new job, Beverly's concerned. Her boss, Audrey, spends little time with her. Beverly keeps busy, but she's not sure she's productive. No one explained the organization's goals and objectives to her, so she can't judge whether her activities align with them. Audrey seems to *assume* Beverly knows what to do. She's given her little guidance. What Beverly *has* learned has come from discussions with others in the office, but many of her co-workers are new also. Beverly wants to understand her goals. She must talk with Audrey, who finally agrees to meet with her. Audrey starts the meeting by telling Beverly she has to leave for the airport, so they'll have to talk fast.

"What's on your mind, Bev?"

"Audrey, I've been here for a month. I'm concerned that you and I have never discussed my job, what you expect, what's important and how you'll measure my performance. How can I do my job if we don't agree on goals?"

"You're doing a great job, Bev. Just do what you've been doing. Our goal's to make money, so if you're helping us do that, everything's fine."

"I know it's important to make money, Audrey, but how do I align my job with that objective? It's too general. I can't relate to it very well."

"Just do your best, Bev, and be productive. Don't waste time on unimportant things, and put in a full day's work. I think those are pretty good goals, don't you?"

"They sound worthwhile, but can you be more specific? I want goals I can measure myself against, goals that will help me know how I'm doing."

"I *told* you you're doing great, Bev. I'm your boss. If I say you're doing great, you don't need to worry."

"Thanks for the compliment, but you're never around. How do you *know* I'm doing great?"

"Don't be ridiculous, Bev. Nobody's complained about you, so you *must* be doing great. Let's get this over with. I need to leave. Now that we've taken care of your questions on goals, is there anything else bothering you?"

"Before you leave, I want to be sure I wrote down the goals you suggested. I have:

1.  Do your best.
2.  Be productive.
3.  Don't waste time.
4.  Put in a full day's work.
5.  Make money.

Is that correct?"

"Sounds good, Bev. You got them right, but 'Make money' should be number one. After all, that's why we're here, isn't it?

"Now you've got goals to work toward. Let's get together next month and see how you're doing with them. I've got to run. This has been a good discussion. Thanks for stopping in."

**C A S E   S T U D Y**

## Questions

- The goals Audrey set for Beverly sound positive. What do you think of them?

- Audrey knew the purpose of her meeting with Beverly was to discuss goals. Can you comment on Audrey's preparation for the meeting?

- How do you think Beverly reacted to the meeting? (Remember, she was told she's "doing a great job.")

- What advice would you give Beverly?

- If you were Audrey's boss and heard about her meeting with Beverly, what would you say to Audrey?

- When Audrey and Beverly get together next month, how will they determine whether Beverly is making progress toward her "goals"? What will they measure?

- If you were holding a goal-setting session with Beverly, what would you do differently?

You may think the previous example is far-fetched. Let me assure you there are thousands of employees in our workforce today who struggle to achieve goals that are just as vague and open-ended as Beverly's. As a manager, resolve never to burden your employees with meaningless goals. Resolve to set goals that are specific, clearly stated and clearly measurable. Remember, sound goals have three identifiable elements:

1. An action verb

2. A measurable result

3. A deadline

## Your Goals

Before discussing how to set goals in delegating to your employees, it's good to review your own goals.

Strong research indicates that goal-oriented individuals are better, more motivated performers. Working toward goals introduces a discipline and provides a framework that lets people make choices with a purpose. Whenever you face a decision, you can choose your course of action depending on whether it matches your goals. With such an approach, goals become powerful forces in your life.

If goals can have such powerful influence, setting them should take high priority. Whether you deal with goals you set for yourself or ones you set with your manager, think carefully about them. If they guide your actions, they deserve special attention.

Think about your goals for your job. Ask yourself the following questions:

- Do I have a clear understanding of my goals?

- Are they written down?

- If so, does my boss have a copy of the same goals?

- Do I agree with my boss on how progress toward my goals will be measured?

> *"I know that you believe you understand what you think I said, but I am not sure you realize that what you heard is not what I meant."*
>
> — *Anonymous*

## EXERCISE

Write below what you feel are your five most important job-related goals in order of priority.

1. _____

_____

_____

2. _____

_____

_____

3. _____

_____

_____

4. _____

_____

_____

5. _____

_____

_____

For each goal, answer the following questions:

- Is the meaning of the goal clear to me?

- Do I understand what is expected of me?

- Will it be obvious when I've reached the goal?

- Do I know how progress will be measured?

- Did I participate in setting the goal, rather than having it dictated to me?

- Is the goal realistic and attainable?

- Does my boss agree with the priority I gave to it?

- Does the goal align with the objectives of my organization?

If you can answer "yes" to all these questions for the five goals you listed, you and your boss make a superb goal-setting team. You should commend yourselves.

If you answered "no" to any of the questions, review the goals carefully. Determine what you lack. Rewrite the unsatisfactory goal(s), keeping in mind the three elements of sound goals:

1) An action verb

2) A measurable result

3) A deadline

When you're satisfied with the rewritten goals, record them on the form below.

## EXERCISE

### Improved Goals

1. _____

_____

_____

2. _____

_____

_____

3. _____

_____

_____

4. _____

_____

_____

5. _____

_____

_____

_Wills Due 11/1_

```
+------------------------------------<Searching: Online Catalog    -- Holdings Display>--------+
!Find...      Options...      Backup      Startover      Quit      Help...:
+------------------------------------------------------------------------------------------------+

        CALL NUMBER: HD 50 H87 1992

            AUTHOR: Huppe, Frank F.

             TITLE: Delegate multiply your impact / written by Frank F.
                    Huppe.

         PUBLISHED: Shawnee Mission, KS (6901 W. 63rd St., Shawnee Mission
                    66201-1349) : National Press Publications, c1992.

       HOLDING CODE: MZ4A

---------------------------------------------------------------------------------------------------
                           LIBRARY HOLDINGS AT
---------------------------------------------------------------------------------------------------

Rockhurst Greenlease Library
1.    CALL NUMBER: HD 50 H87 1992 -- BOOK -- Available
```

End of information for this holding. Type a number for more detail.
                  Press **RETURN** to search the database.

In this exercise, we assumed you *have* job-related goals. If you don't, you need to speak with your boss promptly and ask him or her to work with you to develop some. Otherwise, you'll be like a rudderless ship in a storm. You'll have little to guide you in determining how to spend your time on the job most effectively, and you'll never know what should be delegated.

## Goal-Setting with Your Employees

You can use the exercise you just completed to improve goal-setting with your employees. Give them the same exercise. Ask them to write down their goals. Work through the questions with them. Explain that you want to make sure they have clear goals they understand. Approached properly, this can be an extremely productive interaction between you and your employees. It will help crystallize their thinking about the jobs they do. It will also recharge their enthusiasm because they'll know better how to contribute to the organization's objectives. Furthermore, you'll sharpen your own goal-setting skills.

## Goals in Delegation

Setting goals is an important part of the delegation process. To set them properly, you must know your people and understand how a delegated task will affect them. Be sure you know their strengths, weaknesses, fears and aspirations. A task or goal that fits one employee may be totally wrong for another. Don't choose a delegation goal without considering the delegatee.

*"Our plans miscarry because they have no aim. When a man does not know what harbor he is making for, no wind is the right wind."*

*— Seneca*

*"The human heart has hidden treasures, in secret kept, in silence sealed."*

*— Charlotte Bronte*

## Case Study

Kevin is the new accounting manager, highly regarded and ambitious. He's heard that delegating could make him a better manager, so he's ready to start. He's methodical and well-organized, so he decides to use those skills to set up a "delegation table." After a month, he thinks he knows his new job well enough to delegate tasks and set goals for the four supervisors who report to him — Alice, David, Marie and Tony. Being organized, Kevin chooses four goals, one for each supervisor. That should be fair. He calls a meeting to discuss delegation.

"Delegation is powerful and can help us all become more effective," he says. "When I delegate, I have more time for other activities. And when you take on delegated tasks, you grow and learn. Everybody wins. Please take a copy of my delegation table."

"I've analyzed my job and I've decided which tasks to delegate. They're on the page you just received."

The page Kevin distributed looks like this:

**CASE STUDY**

## DELEGATION TABLE

| GOAL | RESPONSIBILITY |
|------|----------------|
| 1. Evaluate four employment candidates and make hiring recommendations by April 1. | Alice |
| 2. Order three new accounting software packages by June 1. | David |
| 3. Present three talks to professional societies by September 1. | Marie |
| 4. Write four summary reports by October 1. | Tony |

After reading the table, David speaks up. "Those look like excellent goals, but I'm concerned. I've never used computers. I don't even know what software is. Besides, I'll be on military duty during May. I'm not the right person for that goal. Marie could tackle it — she's the computer expert."

Marie replies: "I just started here, Kevin. I've never made a presentation at a society meeting. I've been helping others learn about computers. There's no way I could write and present three talks by September 1! Please give that job to someone else."

Alice speaks up next: "I'm glad about my assignment, Kevin. April 1 is only two weeks away, so I'll start talking to employment candidates tomorrow. I've never interviewed candidates, but I guess you just want to know their ages, their marital status and the number of children. And if I'm in charge, I'll be sure we don't hire any more foreigners! I'm ready."

Kevin isn't sure what to say. Fortunately, Tony speaks up: "Kevin, I was asked to write two talks and present them at the national meeting. I know the topics well, so I was selected. I'm working hard preparing the talks, so I can't write those reports by October 1. Please assign that to someone else."

Kevin hasn't said a word since he passed out the table. He was proud of it — four goals for four people, logically organized. They were clear, easy to understand, and only one goal for each person. He didn't expect such a reaction to his delegation attempt. What went wrong?

### Questions

- Kevin was proud of his delegation table. It seemed to contain all the relevant information: a clearly stated goal, a due date and the responsible person. What else would you have included in the table?

- How well do you think he understood the development needs of his four supervisors?

- How well did Kevin know the skills and capabilities of his people?

- What advice would you give Kevin before he tries delegating again?

## Analysis

Kevin was clearly excited to delegate and saw that effective delegation could help him, his supervisors and the section. He knew it was important to indicate *what* should be done, *who* should do it and *when* it should be completed. However, he didn't consider the *suitability* of the goals for the people he assigned to them.

To delegate effectively, you must learn to match people with *appropriate* goals. To do this, you need to know your people well. If you force an unsuitable goal on an employee, you may totally discourage that person. The result is a disgruntled employee instead of one who grows and develops through the delegation experience. Delegation doesn't mean a mechanical assignment of tasks. It's a process that requires thought, planning and sensitivity. In the next chapter we'll discuss how you can select the right delegatee for the task.

## Knowing Your People

To choose appropriate goals for your people, you must know them well. You need to understand their strengths, weaknesses, hopes and fears. You should know what kinds of special jobs they've done in the past, as well as what challenges and what discourages them. It may seem like a tall order to know your employees that well, but it will pay off.

*"To delegate effectively, you must learn to match people with appropriate goals."*

87

## EXERCISE

On the form below, write the names of all the people who report directly to you. In the columns under "Score," put a number between 1 and 10 in *each* of the columns headed S, W, H and F, indicating how well you think you know each person's strengths, weaknesses, hopes and fears. A "1" means you know practically nothing. A "10" means you think you're very well informed. Add the four numbers for each person and record the sum in the "Total" column. (Such scoring isn't an exact science, but it should help.)

### Knowledge of Employees

| Name | S | W | H | F | Total | Comments |
|------|---|---|---|---|-------|----------|
| 1. _____ | __ | __ | __ | __ | _____ | _____ |
| 2. _____ | __ | __ | __ | __ | _____ | _____ |
| 3. _____ | __ | __ | __ | __ | _____ | _____ |
| 4. _____ | __ | __ | __ | __ | _____ | _____ |
| 5. _____ | __ | __ | __ | __ | _____ | _____ |
| 6. _____ | __ | __ | __ | __ | _____ | _____ |
| 7. _____ | __ | __ | __ | __ | _____ | _____ |

S  =  Strengths
W  =  Weaknesses
H  =  Hopes
F  =  Fears

If your total score for a person is 30 or higher, you've probably made a real effort to get to know him or her. You probably know enough about that person to select appropriate tasks or activities to delegate.

If your total score for a person is less than 30, your understanding of him or her may contain major gaps. Although you might delegate successfully to such people, you should try to increase your knowledge of them to enhance the odds for successful delegation. Pay special attention to any category where you scored less than 5. Try to learn more about that area.

In the column labeled "Comments," record what action to take to learn more about a person. The obvious — and probably best — approach is to talk to the employee! Unfortunately, some managers shrink from trying the direct approach.

If your employees develop confidence and trust in you, they'll feel comfortable discussing their personal goals and ambitions with you. Knowing how they feel about added responsibility is important when developing suitable goals for them.

## Participative Goal-Setting

Kevin's lack of knowledge about his people was the most obvious flaw in his delegation effort. But he made another big mistake. He didn't involve his supervisors during the *planning* phase of the delegation process. He decided what goals he wanted accomplished, then he assigned them. He never discussed his intentions as he planned his delegation table, so he made several assumptions during the planning phase that were wrong.

Talk to your people when you *first* think about delegating a task. Explain what you have in mind and ask for their comments. Two heads are better than one. More often than not, ideas will emerge during the discussion that will help you set better goals. Having participated in setting the goals, your people will be committed to them. Rather than feeling you dumped something on them, they'll feel

> *"What loneliness is more lonely than distrust?"*
>
> — *George Eliot (Mary Ann Evans)*

ownership of the goals and will be more excited about accomplishing them.

If Kevin had involved his people during the planning phase, he would have learned things about their skills, interests, knowledge and schedules that would have prevented him from making inappropriate goal assignments. For example, he would have learned that Alice obviously needs to soften her prejudice against "foreigners" and learn what questions she can ask legally during an interview. Kevin should work with her and perhaps schedule a training course for her. David clearly knows nothing about computers and will be away on military leave for a crucial month. He's *not* the right person to recommend accounting software packages for the section. Marie, however, is a computer expert. She'd be perfect for the software task.

If Kevin had included his people during the planning, he would have learned all these factors so important to making appropriate delegation assignments.

Remember, know your people and include them in planning. It will save you time and lead to better delegation experiences for you and your people.

## Goal-Setting and Challenge

In general, goals should be challenging to provide motivation and a feeling of real accomplishment. You should remember that point when you delegate tasks. However, the following results from motivational research may surprise you.

You might expect that people perform best and get the most satisfaction from their accomplishments when they face the most difficult challenges. In other words, the greater the challenge, the greater the satisfaction. As a general rule, that's true. However, Harvard psychologist David C. McClelland has found that high achievers (10 to 20 percent of the workforce) perform best when they face *moderate* challenges, that is, when they estimate they have

> *"You've got to be very careful if you don't know where you are going, because you might not get there."*
>
> *— Yogi Berra*

90

a 50-50 chance of success. They don't like extremely difficult challenges or ones that don't test their skills at all. They like goals that stretch them a little, but not too much.

McClelland's research results suggest you should set goals in the moderate-to-difficult range in most situations. Through experience with different people, you'll find how much challenge works best.

## Goal-Setting and Control

When you set goals for your employees, you need to make sure that achieving them lies within their control. It's unfair to ask your people to accomplish goals if too many uncontrolled factors may influence the outcome.

For example, suppose you manage a large produce farm and have several workers reporting to you. To help them learn more about the entire farming operation, you decide to delegate. Before you meet with them in January, you jot down the following goals that you feel would improve the farm's output this year:

- Hire three new packers by May 1.

- Purchase one new tractor by February 1.

- Rent three additional trucks by May 1.

- Increase natural rainfall one inch per week by April 1.

- Repair two broken planters by March 1.

Most of these goals are reasonable. If delegated to the right people, they could serve as developmental experiences that would increase their knowledge about the overall farming operation. However, even if you're a city dweller, you should have questioned one of the goals. How would *you* like to be responsible for increasing natural rainfall one inch per week? Unless you have extraordinary powers, that would be an unreasonable goal. To achieve it involves factors beyond your control.

> *"When you set goals for your employees, you need to make sure that achieving them lies within their control."*

When you set ambitious goals to stretch your workers, it's easy to overlook the question of whether they have enough control of the situation to achieve them. Be sure you address that question, because it can be very demoralizing to strive for goals when external factors keep blocking your progress.

---

**Never judge people on results over which they have no control**.

---

This principle is one of the most abused in the workplace. People are often penalized, punished or even discharged for results over which they have no control. Such incidents usually say more about the management than about the punished individual.

As a manager, try to be sensitive and fair — never hold people responsible for results they can't control.

For example, suppose you manage the transportation department and you put Larry in charge of shipping product to your best customer. If he fails to ship in time to meet your customer's deadline because manufacturing can't make the parts, don't blame Larry! He can't control manufacturing, so he can't control the results.

Or suppose you're giving a talk tomorrow morning and you wait till 4 p.m. today to ask your secretary to prepare 10 complicated transparencies for you. She's asked you several times to replace her 10-year-old computer that has no graphics capability, but you always refused. With her inadequate equipment and the time pressure, she'll never get those transparencies done. But don't blame her! She can't control the situation.

*"There is nothing so well known as that we should not expect something for nothing — but we all do..."*

*— Edgar Watson Howe*

## EXERCISE

Earlier in this chapter you made a list of your five most important job-related goals, and then you improved the list. Write the improved list (page 82) again below.

### Job-Related Goals Review

| Goal | Can I Control? | If Not, Why? |
|------|----------------|--------------|
| 1. _____ | _____ | _____ |
| 2. _____ | _____ | _____ |
| 3. _____ | _____ | _____ |
| 4. _____ | _____ | _____ |
| 5. _____ | _____ | _____ |

Review each goal and ask yourself: "Can I really control the factors required for me to achieve this goal?" Think about the steps you must take to achieve it. For each step, consider what you need to do and the barriers you might face. Can you control the factors required for you to progress?

If you answer "no" to either of the questions about your goals, write down *why* you feel you can't control the factors necessary to achieve them. Review each again. If you still feel that way, you may want to discuss the goal with your boss. Perhaps the two of you can modify it to make it more realistic.

Having thought about your own goals, consider those you've delegated to others. Review each one and think about whether your employees can control the factors needed to achieve it. If you suspect they have concerns, encourage them to discuss them with you. Such discussions can strengthen their resolve and renew their commitment to achieving their goals.

## Summary

Setting appropriate goals is vital to any successful delegation effort. When you set goals for your employees:

- Involve them in the planning.

- Be flexible.

- Be realistic.

- Include the three elements of sound goals — action verb, measurable result and deadline.

- Stretch your employees.

- Get their commitment.

*"Success is a journey, not a destination."*

*— Ben Sweetland*

## QUESTIONS FOR PERSONAL DEVELOPMENT

1. What is the major emphasis of this chapter?


2. What do you feel are the most important things you learned from this chapter?

    1)


    2)


    3)


3. How can you apply what you learned to your current job?

    1)


    2)


    3)


4. What objectives will you set for improvement? By when (date)?

    **Objective:**                    **By When?**

    1)


    2)


    3)

5. Who can help you most in applying what you learned in this chapter?

6. What are the major roadblocks that might hinder your progress in applying what you learned in this chapter?

    **Roadblock:**               **Why?**

1)

2)

3)

7. How will you communicate the most important points in this chapter to others in your organization?

8. What preparation is necessary to introduce better delegation?

9. What changes do you expect to make that will better motivate your team?

    **Change:**               **By when?**

1)

2)

3)

10. How will you monitor your progress to assure that performance has improved or productivity has increased? (reports, meetings, etc.)

11. What work-related problems concern you most in evaluating how you will benefit from this chapter?

12. What changes do you expect to see in yourself one year from now as a result of what you learned in this chapter?

# C HAPTER 5

# Choosing a Delegatee

You've analyzed your job and picked the tasks you want to delegate. Now you need to select the appropriate delegatee. Matching the right person to the task is necessary to make your delegation work.

Consider this scenario: "Jim, you've been a medical supply salesman for our company for the past five years. You've done such a good job as a salesman — perfect attendance, punctuality, excellent customer relations skills and knowledge of pharmaceuticals — that we want you to come in next week and be a doctor. So here are the keys to Operating Room 9. Feel free to move in. Now don't worry about a thing. We have confidence in you, and we'll be there all the way to back you up. Just put on this new stethoscope and pick out some supplies for this medical bag. Get a good feel for the job and get to know the nursing staff.

"If this is the job for you, we'll enroll you in a correspondence program through the local college. It's called 'The Theoretical Practice of Medicine.' You'll study medical history, human anatomy and physician penmanship. You'll learn patient billing and how to choose malpractice insurance. After three years, we'll teach you how to operate on people."

Lucky for us, physicians and surgeons aren't trained this way. Yet similar scenarios are played out daily in the business world. Authority is granted to employees precisely because they are so good at their non-authority jobs. But too often the boss forgets to teach them how to do their new jobs.

In many hospitals, for instance, nurses are promoted to department heads with next-to-no training. One day their supervisor tells them, "You're the boss." The next day, they

> *"Authority is granted to employees precisely because they are so good at their non-authority jobs. But too often the boss forgets to teach them how to do their new jobs."*

99

move into a cluttered office and have to figure out what they're supposed to do. Think of the excellent salespeople who get promoted to management and are left to sink or swim.

## Capability Assessment

In order to choose the right person as delegatee for a particular task, you need to analyze and assess the capabilities of your employees. You must give people challenges that fit their next level of growth. An underchallenged person will get bored fast. Overchallenge and you'll have a frustrated, unhappy worker. Mastering this match is more an art than a science, but here's one easy way to improve your accuracy: Look at your people. Who's been hinting for more challenge? Open your mind to people who may not seem qualified — often they have hidden talent you haven't discovered yet. Creative delegation sends a signal that people in your organization can shape their own futures.

The following checklist will help you decide what project to delegate to a particular employee. We'll use it later.

### Work Style Profile

1. Does he work quickly or slowly?
2. Does she seek out new assignments?
3. Does he require minimal or maximum direction?
4. Does she make a lot of mistakes or just a few?
5. Does he write well or poorly?
6. Is she organized or disorganized?
7. Does he like working alone or with others?
8. Does she prefer structured work or the chance for creativity?
9. Does he give strong verbal presentations?
10. Does she handle large assignments well?

As we've mentioned several times, knowing your people well is important for every manager. It's especially important when you want successful delegation results. You know that some tasks require speed, others don't. Some require good oral presentation skills, others can be performed without speaking a word. Some projects demand careful thought and analysis, others are simple and straightforward. When you combine your knowledge of the tasks and your understanding of your employees' capabilities with your purpose for delegating, you

can usually choose the right person. (Note, we did not say the "best" person for the task. We'll discuss that later.)

## EXERCISE

To help you select the right people for delegation, use the following Employee Analysis Chart. It's derived from the 10 questions in the Work Style Profile on the previous page.

In the top row, write the names of all those who report to you. Fill in the columns with answers to the 10 profile questions. For each person, answer the 10 questions and record your answers on the appropriate lines. Choose a word or symbol meaningful to you as a shorthand answer. If you don't know the answer, leave that line blank. The line labeled "Other" is for you to record any additional comments that may help you.

---

### Employee Analysis Chart

| Name: | Ted | ___ | ___ | ___ | ___ | ___ |
|-------|-----|-----|-----|-----|-----|-----|
| 1 | Quick | ___ | ___ | ___ | ___ | ___ |
| 2 | Yes | ___ | ___ | ___ | ___ | ___ |
| 3 | Min | ___ | ___ | ___ | ___ | ___ |
| 4 | Few | ___ | ___ | ___ | ___ | ___ |
| 5 | Well | ___ | ___ | ___ | ___ | ___ |
| 6 | Org | ___ | ___ | ___ | ___ | ___ |
| 7 | ___ | ___ | ___ | ___ | ___ | ___ |
| 8 | Str | ___ | ___ | ___ | ___ | ___ |
| 9 | No* | ___ | ___ | ___ | ___ | ___ |
| 10 | Yes | ___ | ___ | ___ | ___ | ___ |
| Other | Computers | ___ | ___ | ___ | ___ | ___ |

101

We've completed one column of answers (for Ted) as a sample. You can glance at the chart and see that Ted:

1) Works quickly.

2) Seeks out new assignments.

3) Requires minimal direction.

4) Makes few mistakes.

5) Writes well.

6) Is organized.

7) DON'T KNOW.

8) Prefers structured work.

9) Does not give strong verbal presentations.

10) Handles large assignments well.

Other) Is a computer whiz.

When you complete the chart for all your people, you'll have a very useful summary of information about them. Although we've developed the chart primarily as an aid to help you select the right delegatee, you can use it in several other ways. For example, you can refer to it to see what kind of development or training your employees may need. (Note the chart suggests that Ted would benefit from training in verbal presentations.)

After you complete the chart, review it with training or development needs in mind. Put a check by any entry that suggests such a need. (Note the asterisk by "No" on Line 9 for Ted). You can refer to the chart later and follow up on those needs.

## Using the Charts

In Chapter 3 you analyzed your own responsibilities to identify tasks that would be suitable for delegation. You noted them on your Job Activity Analysis form. Now you've completed the Employee Analysis Chart, which provides a summary of key information about your employees' capabilities. These charts complement each other. You can use them together:

### As Delegation Tools

1. Refer to your Job Activity Analysis and identify a task you want to delegate.

2. List the capabilities required in the delegatee to perform the task.

3. Refer to your Employee Analysis Chart to find the person whose capabilities most closely match those required.

4. Delegate the task to the person selected.

### As Development Tools

1. Refer to your Employee Analysis Chart to identify development or training needs you've noted for each employee.

2. Review your Job Activity Analysis to determine whether any tasks you want to delegate could fulfill those development or training needs.

3. If so, delegate the appropriate task to the person with the development need.

## Be Ready for New Ideas

The Job Activity Analysis and Employee Analysis Chart are two aids you can use in delegation and personnel development. But they're not the *only* sources of delegation or development ideas.

As a conscientious manager, you should always be alert to new ideas to improve your delegation skills and to develop your employees. New ideas may come from anywhere — a book, a conversation with a colleague, a walk in the park or a remark by your daughter. Condition yourself to be ready and open for new ideas. Capture them when you first encounter them. You can mull them over, massage them and improve them later. But don't ignore them.

For example, your secretary's casual remark about completing her computer course in night school might trigger a thought — ask her to prepare the sales forecast spreadsheet. Or watching a TV program on outdated manufacturing practices may remind you to delegate the task of recommending new plant equipment purchases. Or listening to a commencement speaker may encourage you to ask someone to write the talk you must present next month. Your mind can make some amazing connections if you just give it a chance.

One trick you may find useful is to carry a small notebook with you *at all times*. Then, if a new idea strikes, jot it down before it gets away. You can decide later whether to work with it or discard it. But capture it, don't lose it. It may not return.

## Objectives in Selecting Delegatees

Selection of delegatees includes three general objectives. Weigh these objectives to determine which goals are most important to the task at hand. The person you select must be competent, but you must consider other factors as well. The three general objectives to consider when choosing a delegatee are:

1.  **Direct Results**. For most cases of delegation, the direct result is the most important objective.

    Mr. Addison of Acme Supply has called demanding to know where his 600 cases of widgets are. If the missing widgets are not accounted for within 24 hours, he's threatening to cancel the order. Both Sharon and Sam know how to track the missing widgets. However, Sharon has more experience at tracking diverted orders, plus she's dealt directly with Mr. Addison and his secretary in the past. So, even though Sam could do the job, you opt for

Sharon this time. She's obviously more proficient and better suited to this particular delegation opportunity.

2. **Development**. Development of employee skills always represents an important delegation goal. It also complicates the selection of the delegatee. You want the right person, not necessarily the most competent person. Surprisingly, numerous delegation opportunities crop up where the objective of developing the delegatee's skills is paramount and the direct result matters less. Look for tasks with results that are not critical or urgent. Identify jobs where a few minor mistakes won't cause serious problems, then delegate them. People normally half-dead from boredom or frustration at the office come alive when given a new challenge, and their abilities take a major leap.

   Realizing that Mr. Addison of Acme Supply is a major customer, you know your entire staff must handle his account with proper concern and respect. From the first day that Sam joins your staff as an accounting clerk/typist, you begin to explain the importance of the Acme account. Even though Sharon can handle these routine transactions of billing, shipping and accounting for the Acme orders because she's done it for years, you begin to delegate the Acme transactions to Sam. Eventually, Mr. Addison will call with a rush order or a "temper tantrum" as he is prone to do. When the crisis comes, Sam will be ready to respond because you've developed his skills slowly, but surely.

3. **Evaluation**. Sooner or later your employees will have to be tested under fire. In some delegations, your main objective is to watch individual performance in a given situation. Be careful not to delegate with the expectation of failure, but know that delegation reveals employee strengths and weaknesses that may not otherwise be apparent.

   The manager of a local food brokerage firm needs to fill an account representative's position. To test his secretary's skill for the job, he asks her to help an experienced account representative set up a brand new supermarket. They accomplish the job in an acceptable

> *"Practice yourself in little things, and then proceed to greater."*
>
> *— Epictetus*

manner, but the secretary realizes that this job is not for her. The working conditions, travel, hours and other things are not what she wants. Both she and her boss can make important long-term assessments based on this delegation.

Delegation is a useful tool to determine the potential of employees in the workforce. It's mutually beneficial to let employees explore all facets of the work done in your business.

## Selecting the Right Person

As a manager, your natural tendency is to try to complete a task rapidly and accurately. You want results, and you want to achieve them as efficiently as possible. That's your job. So, when you delegate a task, you instinctively think of your star performer, the person you know is best for the job. But remember, the *best* person isn't always the *right* person. Choosing the right person in delegating is extremely important, so let's explore that issue further.

Managers who focus on short-term results instead of long-term planning are usually the ones who pick the best person, but not necessarily the right person. When you think about it, that's not surprising.

If you focus on the short-term and don't worry much about the future, developing your people is probably not a high priority for you. Because development *aims* at the future, it's not something you do in a day. It's not a one-shot deal. It's a process that takes time and effort.

As you've just learned, you should consider three general objectives in selecting delegatees:

1. Direct results — getting the job done

2. Development — helping an employee acquire greater skills

3. Evaluation — observing an employee's performance

> *"I hold that man in the right who is most closely in league with the future."*
>
> — *Henrik Ibsen*

If you focus only on direct results, you'll almost always delegate to your star performer because:

- You're almost certain to get the results you want

- There's little risk for you

- It takes less time and effort

But there are hazards.

As you learn more about delegating and your skill and confidence increase, you'll identify more tasks and activities to delegate. As the list grows, your need to delegate will increase. If you're concerned only with direct results, you'll probably turn to your best person every time for the reasons mentioned above. So what happens?

At first, your star performer will appreciate the tasks you delegate because he or she recognizes that they present opportunities for growth. However, if you continue to pile tasks on these employees, they'll grow to resent it. Their performance will suffer, and the direct results you expected may never materialize.

While your star performer is getting more displeased, the rest of your people will also become unhappy. They may view your actions as obvious favoritism. They'll wonder why you don't recognize *their* development needs by delegating to *them*. Their performance, too, may decline. So, by focusing exclusively on direct results, your delegation efforts may actually *lower* the overall effectiveness of the group. You certainly don't want that to happen.

We presented the three general objectives in delegatee selection as separate and distinct, but you can use more than one of them in any given act of delegation. You don't necessarily delegate *only* for direct results or *only* for development or *only* for evaluation. Frequently, you want to achieve two of the objectives or even all three. If one act of delegation can achieve the direct results, help develop an employee and let you evaluate a person, that's a bonus. As you become more experienced in delegating, you'll learn how to multiply your impact each time you delegate.

> *"You don't necessarily delegate only for direct results or only for development or only for evaluation. Frequently, you want to achieve two of the objectives or even all three."*

## EXERCISE

Consider yourself the manager in each of the following cases. Assume you've asked an employee to complete a project or perform a task. What might you accomplish in each of the three general objectives through your delegation?

**Case #1.** You manage a small hardware store. On several occasions when you've been away from the store, you've left Richard in charge. He's ready for more responsibility. You ask him to close the store for the night, lock up the building and deposit the receipts at the bank. What might you hope to accomplish in each general area?

1.  Direct results

    _____

    _____

    _____

2.  Development

    _____

    _____

    _____

3.  Evaluation

    _____

    _____

    _____

## EXERCISE (Continued)

**Case #2.** You manage an accounting section in a large firm. Although Helen was hired as a clerk/typist, she seems capable of greater responsibility and is eager to learn. She recently told you she's taking a computer course at night. You ask her to assemble the section's monthly cost figures and then enter them on a spreadsheet for the quarterly report. What might you hope to accomplish in each general area?

1. Direct results

   _____

   _____

   _____

2. Development

   _____

   _____

   _____

3. Evaluation

   _____

   _____

   _____

**EXERCISE (Continued)**

**Case #3.** You manage a group of volunteers for a nonprofit charitable agency. They spend most of their time answering phones and mailing out information. However, Dorothy has demonstrated excellent speaking skills and good rapport with several benefactors who have visited the office. She's also shown interest in joining your regular staff as a paid employee. You ask her to prepare a 15-minute program about the agency and present it to two local civic groups. What might you hope to accomplish in each general area?

1.  Direct results

    _____

    _____

    _____

2.  Development

    _____

    _____

    _____

3.  Evaluation

    _____

    _____

    _____

## EXERCISE (Continued)

**Case #4.** You manage a group of research engineers in an electronics company. One of your customers is having problems with a digital relay he buys from you. The marketing people who usually deal with him haven't been able to solve the problem. Jack is one of your best engineers and troubleshooters, but he hasn't dealt directly with customers. You ask him to visit the customer, analyze the problem and recommend a solution. What might you hope to accomplish in each general area?

1.   Direct results

_____

_____

_____

2.   Development

_____

_____

_____

3.   Evaluation

_____

_____

_____

## Selecting Delegatees for Your Tasks

You've put substantial effort into preparing your Job Activity Analysis (Chapter 3) and the Employee Analysis Chart (this chapter). Now you'll use them to help you choose delegatees for actual tasks on your list.

A form called "Task Analysis and Delegatee Selection" is reproduced three times on the following pages. You'll use these forms to analyze three tasks you want to delegate and then choose the delegatee.

### Instructions

Refer to your Job Activity Analysis and pick three important tasks you've identified as suitable for delegation. Then refer to the Employee Analysis Chart to help you complete the form. Using one form for *each* task, complete each form as follows:

1. Write a few words to describe the task or activity.

2. Summarize the *direct results* required to consider the task or activity completed.

3. List your employees who could achieve the direct results.

4. Indicate which employee you feel is the *best* person for the task. Who is *most likely* to achieve the direct results because of experience, capability, motivation, etc.?

5. If achieving direct results is not your only objective, consider whether the task or activity could be used to *develop* an employee. If so, list those who would benefit from such a development experience.

6. If achieving direct results is not your only objective, consider whether the task or activity could be used to *evaluate* an employee. If so, list those you could evaluate with such a task.

7. After considering all the relevant factors suggested to you, choose the *right* person for the task or activity and record his or her name.

## EXERCISE

### Task Analysis and Delegatee Selection I

1. Task/Activity:_____

2. **Direct results** required:
   a)_____
   b)_____
   c)_____

3. Employees who could achieve **direct results**:
   a)_____
   b)_____
   c)_____

4. "BEST" person for the task/activity (most likely to achieve **direct results**):

   _____

5. Person for whom task/activity could be used for **development**:
   a)_____
   b)_____
   c)_____

6. Person for whom task/activity could be used for **evaluation**:
   a)_____
   b)_____
   c)_____

7. "RIGHT" person for the task/activity considering the direct results required and the other factors listed above:

   _____

## EXERCISE (Continued)

### Task Analysis and Delegatee Selection II

1.  Task/Activity:_____

2.  **Direct results** required:

    a)_____

    b)_____

    c)_____

3.  Employees who could achieve **direct results**:

    a)_____

    b)_____

    c)_____

4.  "BEST" person for the task/activity (most likely to achieve **direct results**):

    _____

5.  Person for whom task/activity could be used for **development**:

    a)_____

    b)_____

    c)_____

6.  Person for whom task/activity could be used for **evaluation**:

    a)_____

    b)_____

    c)_____

7.  "RIGHT" person for the task/activity considering the direct results required and the other factors listed above:

    _____

## EXERCISE (Continued)

# Task Analysis and Delegatee Selection III

1.  Task/Activity:_____

2.  **Direct results** required:

    a)_____

    b)_____

    c)_____

3.  Employees who could achieve **direct results**:

    a)_____

    b)_____

    c)_____

4.  "BEST" person for the task/activity (most likely to achieve **direct results**):

    _____

5.  Person for whom task/activity could be used for **development**:

    a)_____

    b)_____

    c)_____

6.  Person for whom task/activity could be used for **evaluation**:

    a)_____

    b)_____

    c)_____

7.  "RIGHT" person for the task/activity considering the direct results required and the other factors listed above:

    _____

C A S E  S T U D Y

> *"Don't be afraid to take a big step if one is indicated. You can't cross a chasm in two small jumps."*
>
> — *Lloyd George*

The "Task Analysis and Delegatee Selection" form offers a logical and systematic approach to choosing delegatees. However, sometimes you may have a "gut" feeling about someone. You may sense a hidden talent and want to delegate to a person whose name didn't appear anywhere on the form you completed. If so, go for it. Follow your instincts. You'll probably be quite pleased with the outcome. Besides, delegation isn't an exact science. Take a chance. Your employee may surprise you. Remember, the more often you delegate, the easier it will get. Your skill will grow with experience.

**Case Study**

Barbara is office manager for a graphics firm. She oversees four people with a wide variety of duties. Her boss, Mr. Laird, told her he wants the office operation to run smoothly. That's her primary responsibility. He's delegated authority so she can order any equipment and supplies she needs. He insists she develop her people, but he hasn't explained what he means by that.

Barbara is conscientious and wants to be a good manager. She knows she must please Mr. Laird, get the job done, develop her people and continue to grow and develop herself. Recently she learned about delegation, and she's determined to delegate and increase the effectiveness of her staff.

First, she analyzes her job to identify tasks she could delegate. Without considering to whom she might delegate them, she lists the following tasks for possible delegation:

1.  Evaluate a new messenger service to deliver layouts.

2.  Order coffee and doughnuts for the weekly staff meeting.

3.  Prepare the daily absentee report for Mr. Laird.

4.  Write the monthly group accomplishment report.

5.  Present a talk about office support jobs to a group of students.

6. Prepare a detailed directory of services offered by the office support staff.

7. Make arrangements for Tina's wedding reception at the country club. (Tina is Mr. Laird's daughter.)

8. Design a new logo for the company's stationery.

9. Select and order a new intercom system for the office.

Anne, Bill, Charlie and Debra all report to Barbara. She's worked with them for six months and feels she knows them well. She wants to help them develop and plans to use delegation.

She now has a list of items to delegate and wants to assign them. From her knowledge of the four workers, she uses the Work Style Profile to complete the Employee Analysis Chart on the following pages to help her delegate to the right people.

Assume you are Barbara and complete the Delegation Summary Chart on page 119, using your knowledge of the people summarized on the Employee Analysis Chart.

The first column on the Delegation Summary Chart contains a few words to identify each task. In the second column, record the name of the person you feel is the "right" person for the job. In the third column, give your reason(s) for selecting that person.

(In an actual situation, you'd have information about your four employees *in addition to* what is found in the Employee Analysis Chart. However, try to use the Chart to guide your decisions.)

If, after studying the Employee Analysis Chart, you decide not to delegate a particular task to any of the four, write "NO ONE" in the second column and give your reason(s).

## EXERCISE

---

### Employee Analysis Chart

#### WORK STYLE PROFILE

| WORK STYLE | ANNE | BILL | CHARLIE | DEBRA |
|---|---|---|---|---|
| 1 Does he work quickly or slowly? | Quick | Slow | Quick | Slow |
| 2 Does she seek out new assignments? | No | Yes | Yes | No |
| 3 Does he require minimal or maximum direction? | Min | Min | Max | Min |
| 4 Does she make a lot of mistakes or just a few? | Few | | Many | Few |
| 5 Does he write well or poorly? | Well | Well | | Poor |
| 6 Is she organized or disorganized? | Org | Dis | Org | |
| 7 Does he like working alone or with others? | Others | | Alone | Alone |
| 8 Does she prefer structured work or the chance for creativity? | Creat | Str | Str | Creat |
| 9 Does he give strong verbal presentations? | | Yes | | Yes |
| 10 Does she handle large assignments well? | Yes | No | No | Yes |
| Other............................................. | 1 | | 2 | 3 |

*1 - Teaches art on weekends*
*2 - Electronics genius*
*3 - Attends night school*

**EXERCISE**

## BARBARA'S DELEGATION SUMMARY CHART

| TASK | DELEGATE TO | REASON |
|------|-------------|--------|
| 1. Messenger service | _____ | _____ |
| 2. Coffee/doughnuts | _____ | _____ |
| 3. Absentee report | _____ | _____ |
| 4. Accomp. report | _____ | _____ |
| 5. Talk to students | _____ | _____ |
| 6. Directory of services | _____ | _____ |
| 7. Tina's reception | _____ | _____ |
| 8. New logo | _____ | _____ |
| 9. New intercom | _____ | _____ |

**Questions**

- Were there any tasks on Barbara's list for which the Employee Analysis Chart offered little relevant information? If so, which one(s)?

  _____

  _____

  _____

  _____

- Were there any tasks on the list you feel are totally inappropriate for delegation?
  If so, which one(s)? Why?

  _____

  _____

  _____

  _____

- Was the information in the "Other" entries of any value in choosing the right delegatee? If so, in what way?

  _____

  _____

  _____

  _____

## Summary

Remember, people are tremendously diverse. Your employees have different strengths, weaknesses, skills, aspirations and needs. It's your job to recognize those characteristics and blend them into your overall actions as a manager. Delegation is a great way to address needs — yours, theirs and the organization's. By choosing your delegatees carefully and selecting the *right* ones, you can strengthen your employees' skills and significantly shape the future of your entire organization. It takes more thought during the planning phase to decide on the right person for the job, but the results are worth the effort.

Even employees who resist new assignments can and should be delegated to. It's your responsibility to define tasks that fall within the scope of that person's existing abilities and that reasonably stretch his skills in the training process. So, we come right back to the basis of delegation: your ability to define jobs and creatively match those jobs to your staff.

## QUESTIONS FOR PERSONAL DEVELOPMENT

1. What is the major emphasis of this chapter?

2. What do you feel are the most important things you learned from this chapter?

    1)

    2)

    3)

3. How can you apply what you learned to your current job?

    1)

    2)

    3)

*"If the primary aim of a captain were to preserve his ship, he would keep it in port forever."*

*— Thomas Aquinas*

4. What objectives will you set for improvement? By when (date)?

   **Objective:**                                    **By When?**

   1)

   2)

   3)

5. Who can help you most in applying what you learned in this chapter?

6. What are the major roadblocks that might hinder your progress in applying what you learned in this chapter?

   **Roadblock:**                                    **Why?**

   1)

   2)

   3)

7. How will you communicate the most important points in this chapter to others in your organization?

8. What preparation is necessary to introduce better delegation?

9. What changes do you expect to make that will better motivate your team?

   **Change:**                    **By when?**

   1)

   2)

   3)

10. How will you monitor your progress to assure that performance has improved or productivity has increased? (reports, meetings, etc.)

11. What work-related problems concern you most in evaluating how you will benefit from this chapter?

12. What changes do you expect to see in yourself one year from now as a result of what you learned in this chapter?

# C HAPTER 6

# Developing People Through Delegation

You've learned that you must consider several factors when you delegate — the task itself, your purpose and choosing the right employee. By wise choice of the right task, purpose and employee, you can achieve the results you need, as well as develop and evaluate your people. In this chapter we'll focus on the second purpose, developing people through delegation.

Let's clarify one important point. As a manager, you've often heard that one of your primary responsibilities is to develop your people. That statement is *almost* correct. To get it right, let's modify it this way:

> **As a manager, your responsibility is to provide a climate that enables and encourages your people *to develop themselves.***

You really can't develop someone else. You can help, encourage, persuade, push, coax and cajole others, but they must develop *themselves.* Your job as manager is to provide a climate that lets them do that.

We'll talk a lot about managers developing people. Just remember that's a shorthand way of saying managers provide a climate that enables and encourages people to develop themselves.

125

Delegation not only helps you get a job done, it often gives you a great chance to develop your people. Be alert and sensitive to your people's needs, and you'll recognize development chances when they occur. Do they need to write more clearly, speak more effectively, learn to use computers or organize their projects better? If so, delegate tasks that will help them develop these skills.

Be proactive and *create* delegation situations that you can convert to growth opportunities. Launch a newsletter and ask your people to write sections of it. Appoint an editor and charge him or her with organizing all the material. Encourage the clerical staff to use the new word-processing software to prepare the text. By clever choice of project, you can create development opportunities for several people. Unless you're totally self-centered, you'll get great satisfaction from helping your people and watching them grow. For most managers, that's one of the biggest rewards of the job.

Keep in mind that you must know your people well to develop them successfully through delegation. Talk to them. Listen to what they say. Work with them to identify paths for growth. Learn their personal and job-related needs. Delegate tasks that contribute to their growth and satisfy those needs. It takes time and effort to get to know your people well, but that's the key to successful delegation.

## Development Never Stops

Developing your people should be an ongoing process. It's not something that's finished tomorrow or next week. *Every* employee in your organization can — and should — continue to learn, grow and develop. No matter how well we do our jobs, all of us need to improve in some areas. As the manager, you must nurture and encourage everyone to strive for improvement. You must demonstrate by your actions that you *want* to help your people.

A continuously improving organization is vibrant. You can spot a can-do attitude in its members. They always look for ways to improve as individuals and as an organization. On the other hand, people or organizations that feel they don't need to learn or grow more will soon stagnate. They'll become

*"The only thing necessary for the triumph of evil is for good men to do nothing."*

*— Edmund Burke*

bored and boring. While they congratulate themselves for reaching their final state of growth, the competition will pass them by.

One of the most important things you can do as manager is be the spark that ignites the flame of continuous improvement in your people. You can:

1. Tell them you're committed to help them.

2. Work with them individually to find specific ways they can continue to develop and improve themselves.

3. Show by your own self-improvement that you understand the benefits of continual growth by reading, taking courses, etc.

4. Continue to stretch your people with challenging but realistic goals.

Belonging to an organization in which the manager encourages continual growth and development is exciting and motivating. Be that spark. Create such an environment for your people. Chances are you'll like the results.

> *"One of the strongest characteristics of genius is the power of lighting its own fire."*
>
> *—John Foster*

## EXERCISE

Consider the environment in your organization and your own
attitudes toward growth and development. By looking at what
inspires and blocks your own self-improvement goals, you can
better understand how to help your people grow. Complete
the following worksheet:

- Set clear goals for your own development. Write
  down your most important goals.

  Example: Take a public speaking course by
  December 31

1._____

_____

2._____

_____

3._____

_____

• Does your organization support your efforts to reach your self-improvement goals? The following checklist will help you assess that environment.

## EXERCISE

### Checklist

|  |  | YES | NO |
|---|---|---|---|
| 1) | Does your manager meet with you regularly to discuss your self-improvement goals? | ___ | ___ |
| 2) | Does your manager delegate assignments that help you achieve your goals? | ___ | |
| 3) | Does your manager encourage you to take self-improvement courses? | ___ | ___ |
| 4) | Does your organization pay for such courses? | ___ | ___ |
| 5) | Does your organization purchase self-improvement materials for you (books, tapes, etc.)? | ___ | ___ |
| 6) | Does your organization have a reading room or library where you can borrow self-improvement materials? | ___ | ___ |
| 7) | Does your manager provide counseling and assistance in setting personal goals or arrange for someone else to help you? | ___ | ___ |

## EXERCISE (Continued)

- If your organization does *not* support your efforts to reach your self-improvement goals, what do you need?

  _____

  _____

  _____

  _____

- What changes would you recommend to improve the organization's environment for helping you reach your self-improvement goals?

  1. _____

     _____

  2. _____

     _____

  3. _____

     _____

- Do you feel you support your own people's efforts to grow and develop?

  If so, write down the things you do that show your commitment and support.

  1. _____

     _____

  2. _____

     _____

  3. _____

     _____

## Delegation and Continuous Improvement

As you learn to use delegation more effectively, you become a stronger manager and your people grow and develop. The capability of the entire organization improves. As you practice your skills and learn more about delegation, you should continue to improve. It's an ongoing process. Look upon it as a process of *continuous improvement.*

The concept of continuous improvement reaches far beyond delegation. Entire books have been written about it, and Japan has risen to economic prominence by fierce dedication to it. Because it's such an important concept, especially in today's competitive arena, you should know about it.

The Japanese word *kaizen* means *ongoing improvement* that involves everyone — top management, managers and workers. More broadly, the kaizen philosophy assumes that your entire way of life — be it working life, social life or home life — deserves to be continuously improved. Although the concept of continuous improvement is simple, dedicated application of it can be extremely powerful. The kaizen strategy is generally seen today as the single most important concept in Japanese management and the key to Japan's competitive success.

You know the saying, "If it ain't broke, don't fix it," that is very popular in the United States. In contrast, you could paraphrase the kaizen philosophy as:

> **"If it ain't broke, fix it anyway and make it better."**

Don't be satisfied with the status quo. Always look for ways to improve yourself and your organization.

*"As you practice your skills and learn more about delegation, you should continue to improve ... Look upon it as a process of continuous improvement."*

## Continuous Improvement and Empowerment

In the preface to his popular book, *Zapp!,* William C. Byham writes:

> "More and more in years to come, the successful organizations will be the ones best able to apply the creative energy of individuals toward constant improvement. Yet, constant improvement is a value that cannot be imposed upon people. It has to come from the individual. The only way to get people to adopt constant improvement as a way of life in doing daily business is by *empowering* them."
>
> (Taken from *Zapp! The Lightning of Empowerment* by William C. Byham with Jeff Cox. Copyright Development Dimension International, Inc., 1989. Used with permission.)

You can't force your employees to adopt continuous or "constant" improvement as a way of life. But you can create an environment that encourages them to take personal interest in improving the organization. You must also train them properly. That's empowerment.

## Everyone Must Participate

To make continuous improvement efforts work, you must involve everyone in the organization. You won't achieve full benefits unless everyone commits to the concept and its use. Continuous improvement has been launched in some companies by middle managers who embraced its potential, but lacked support from top management. Such attempts usually fail. You must commit significant resources of people, time and money to achieve the full impact of continuous improvement. To sustain the commitment of resources, top management must *drive* the effort. Mere approval isn't enough. The push *must* come from the top.

To achieve the full impact, top management must introduce continuous improvement as a corporate strategy and show commitment to it. Middle management must set the goals in motion as directed by top management. Supervisors must make plans and guide workers. The workers must engage in continuous improvement through individual and group activities. *Everyone* must be involved.

*" ... You can create an environment that encourages (employees) to take personal interest in improving the organization ... That's empowerment."*

Continuous improvement must not be perceived as "the program of the month." Instead, it must become a way of life for the entire organization, spreading through all activities. People must believe they can improve themselves and their organization. You must provide a climate where continuous improvement is encouraged and practiced.

Much of the power of continuous improvement comes from having an organization of people who don't like the current situation, *whatever* it is. Sounds like a nightmare, right? What sensible manager would want to work in such an environment? That depends on the attitude and motivation of the people. Two individuals can observe the same situation and both feel dissatisfied. However, they'll react very differently because of their own attitudes and motivation. An employee interested in continuous improvement is more likely to come up with a solution to a problem. Consider the following example.

### Example

Mail service in the building has been slipping for several weeks. Mail used to be delivered to the third-floor offices by 10 a.m. every morning. Last week it wasn't delivered till after 3 p.m., and on Friday it never was delivered at all. There was noticeable grumbling on the third floor and general dissatisfaction throughout the building with the mail service.

First thing Monday, Doug marched into his manager's office.

"I'm really fed up with the mail service around here, Terry. Those idiots in the mail room can't deliver anything on time. When I call down there to complain, they're too busy sorting mail to talk to me. I've been expecting some important letters, but they'll probably lose them before they even get them delivered. Why do you hire such incompetents to work in this building? They must have negative IQs. This is worse than the mail service in the job I just left."

On Tuesday morning, Gene stopped in to talk with Terry.

> *"To be what we are and to become what we are capable of becoming, is the only end of life."*
>
> — *Robert Louis Stevenson*

Example

"Terry, I'm concerned about the deterioration in our mail service lately. I think we need to correct the situation, so I've taken some action. I talked to the supervisor in the mail room to find out what's causing the delays. She says there are really two problems. One of her people is in the hospital, and the central mail office is no longer doing any preliminary sorting. She has to sort everything after it gets to our building. I offered to help her locate some temporary workers till Larry gets out of the hospital. I also talked with the central mail office and convinced the people there to resume preliminary sorting of the mail. Things should be back on track tomorrow."

Doug and Gene were both third-floor residents who were unhappy with the mail service and decided to discuss the situation with their manager. The similarities end there.

Doug was belligerent and quick to blame the workers in the mail room. He was also unkind and insulting. He was determined to complain about the existing situation, but made no attempt to find the cause or seek a solution.

Gene was also dissatisfied, but he checked into the situation to determine what (not *who*) was causing the problem. He also looked for ways to *improve* the situation. His goal was not to blame people for the problems but rather to see how he could help correct them. So you see how two dissatisfied people with very different attitudes and motivation reacted to the same problem.

In this example, something clearly was "broken" and needed to be "fixed." Continuous improvement of an organization requires that you address such problems and correct them. As a manager, you need to correct them or see that someone else does.

*"You should also work to improve conditions even when you don't see any problems."*

## If It Ain't Broke, Fix It Anyway

You should try to correct problems wherever they exist in your organization. But you should also work to improve conditions even when you *don't* see any problems. Let's return to our revised saying:

**"If it ain't broke, fix it anyway
and make it better."**

What does that mean in a continuous-improvement environment? Let's look at another example.

## Example

Mary's holding a staff meeting to advise her sales force of new procedures.

"Your new order forms now contain four pages — the white original you send to the plant, the blue copy you send to accounting, the yellow copy you send to inventory control and the pink copy you keep for your files. Remember, as soon as you take an order, mail those first three copies to their destinations immediately. We don't have them yet, but preprinted envelopes with the addresses of the plant, accounting and inventory control will be available next week. They're color-coded, so just use the blue envelope for the blue form, yellow envelope for the yellow form and so on. Keep track of your postage costs and include them in your weekly expense account. Any questions?"

"Yes, Mary, I have one. Aren't the accounting and inventory control offices located *in the plant building?*"

"Yes, Mark, they are. Why do you ask?"

"Why should we pay postage to mail *three* separate envelopes when we could mail all the forms to the plant in *one* envelope? Then they could be delivered using our internal mail service."

"That's a good suggestion, Mark. Let's follow up on that. What do the rest of you think?"

"I think Mark's idea would be a definite improvement," said Linda, "but I'd like the group to consider another possibility. You told us last week, Mary, that we needed to get our orders into the plant faster if we're going to keep up with our competition. Mail can be slow and unreliable. Why don't we just fax our orders to the plant? It costs a little more, but getting the order filled more rapidly should be worth it."

"That's a great idea, Linda. Let's try that for a while to see how it works.

**Example**

"I'm pleased with your suggestions today. The colored-envelope approach works fine in region 5 and would probably be adequate for us, too. However, you've obviously looked for ways to improve on that approach to make us more competitive. That's great! Thanks for keeping continuous improvement in mind."

That's a small example, but you get the message. Encourage your people to seek better ways of doing things in all aspects of their jobs. Never be satisfied with the status quo. Support one another as you try to find better approaches. The resulting improvements will benefit the entire organization.

## The Manager's Role

Even if you don't have a full-blown continuous-improvement effort under way in your company, you can use continuous-improvement approaches to strengthen your own organization. As the manager, try to:

- Empower your people.

- Encourage them to suggest improvements in all aspects of their jobs.

- Arrange for training so they can learn to use continuous-improvement approaches.

- Delegate with continuous improvement in mind.

If you have the chance, attend a continuous-improvement training program yourself. Knowledge of the techniques is useful even though your organization may not use them widely. If continuous improvement impresses you when you're exposed more fully to it, you may want to encourage your top management to look into it as a strategy. Be prepared for resistance or lack of interest. Remember that a complete continuous-improvement effort requires *major* commitment from top management. You won't find that in many organizations. However, if you become convinced of the value and potential of continuous improvement, talk it up with your colleagues. If possible, tell your top management of your convictions and why you believe continuous improvement

*"Encourage your people to seek better ways of doing things ... Never be satisfied with the status quo."*

would be good for your organization. You may be the spark that ignites enthusiasm for continuous improvement within your top management. No one questions that continuous improvement is a good thing and that every organization should try to improve. However, few members of top management are willing to commit themselves, their time and their resources to make continuous improvement an all-pervasive effort throughout their organizations.

## Delegate with Continuous Improvement in Mind

How do you link continuous improvement to delegation?

Fundamentally, delegation is a technique *aimed* at improvement. When you completed the Job Activity Analysis on page 51, you identified tasks you must do yourself and tasks you can delegate. After learning more about what and what not to delegate, you returned to your list of activities and revised it. You can do this several times as your knowledge of delegation grows. You're engaged in continuous improvement of your job definition. You do this to become a better manager. Hopefully you'll commit to revisit your Job Analysis periodically and update it so you can keep improving your managerial skills and capability.

You don't delegate, of course, to improve only yourself. You've learned the importance of delegation as a way to develop your people. By matching their needs with tasks you want to delegate you help them improve. They grow with completion of each delegated task, so you encourage their continuous improvement each time you delegate to them. Never tell yourself that your people are now "fully improved." Keep stretching them so that continuous improvement is ingrained in your contact with them.

What about the notion of knowing your people well enough to make good delegation choices? That, too, involves continuous improvement. As you work with your people, you should continue to improve your knowledge of them. If you delegate a task to Karen today and follow up as she progresses toward its completion, you'll learn more about her as a person and as an employee. That lets you pick an even more appropriate task for

> *"Delegation is a technique aimed at improvement."*

her next time. For example, if you ask her to write a report, you may learn that she organizes details very well. Next time you can delegate a large task that lets her use her organizational skills and that develops them further. By working with your people, you continue to improve your knowledge of them and your understanding of their needs.

By developing the right outlook toward delegation, you can make every delegated task a continuous-improvement experience for yourself and usually for other people, too. Start out by consciously asking yourself, "How can I make this a continuous-improvement experience for me and the employee?" After a while, you won't have to ask the question. Your delegations will automatically become continuous-improvement experiences for you as well as for your people.

## EXERCISE

While completing this worksheet, consider your own working style and the procedures you use often.

- When was the last time you modified any process or procedure to improve it?

  _____

- What changes did you make?

  _____
  _____
  _____

- Since making those changes, have you thought of additional ways to Improve the process or procedure? If so, what have you done to put them into action?

  _____
  _____
  _____
  _____

- Do you ever hold continuous-improvement sessions with your staff to identify ways to improve how your organization operates?

  _____

  If so, describe the response from your people (cooperative, interested, eager, reluctant, bored, etc.).

  _____
  _____
  _____
  _____

- Does your company or organization have a formal continuous-improvement effort? If so, do you consider it successful?

  _____

## The Manager's Expectations

Many managers unintentionally treat their people in a way that leads to second-rate performance. They ignore when they should encourage them. They reprimand when they should support them. They talk when they should listen. They fail to recognize their employees' needs. The way you treat your people is subtly influenced by what you expect of them. If your expectations are low, productivity will likely be low. In George Bernard Shaw's play *Pygmalion*, Professor Henry Higgins takes a flower girl, Eliza Doolittle, and turns her into "a lady" by training her in speaking, walking, dressing and etiquette. At one point, Eliza speaks to one of Professor Higgins' friends and reflects on the different ways he and Professor Higgins treat her:

> "You see, really and truly, apart from the things anyone can pick up (the dressing and the proper way of speaking and so on) the difference between a lady and a flower girl is not how she behaves, but how she's treated. I shall always be a flower girl to Professor Higgins, because he always treats me as a flower girl and always will, but I know I can be a lady to you, because you always treat me as a lady and always will."

J. Sterling Livingston of the Harvard Business School describes the "Pygmalion-in-Management Effect" this way:

1. **What a manager expects of a person and how he treats the person will profoundly influence the person's performance and career progress.** What's critical in communicating expectations is not what a boss says, but what is done. Indifference and noncommittal treatment communicates low expectations and leads to inferior performance.

2. **Superior managers create high performance expectations that people can fulfill.** People will not strive for high productivity unless they consider the boss's high expectations realistic and achievable. If they are pushed to strive for unattainable goals, they eventually give up trying. Frustrated, they settle for results that are lower than they are capable of achieving.

> *"The worst sin towards our fellow creatures is not to hate them, but to be indifferent to them; that's the essence of inhumanity."*
>
> *— George Bernard Shaw*

## The Importance of Self-Esteem

To delegate successfully, you must recognize the importance of your employees' self-esteem. It's a major factor in how they respond to delegation. Many psychological studies have shown that when a person's self-esteem is threatened, he becomes distressed. This acts as a barrier to delegation because the distressed person is reluctant to accept additional responsibility. As a manager, you need to recognize the importance of your employees' self-esteem and strive to strengthen it. People with strong self-esteem are motivated to accomplish their goals.

The idea of self-esteem as a motivator is pretty recent. In the 1930s, the issue was irrelevant. Then the issues were money, security and survival — the things that were in short supply. After the depression of the 1930s, the country moved into a period of sustained economic growth. For most people, basic security and survival needs were met. Periods of minor recession occurred, but the overall trend resulted in greater prosperity for most people. Once their basic needs were met, people were motivated by a new set of drives. They became more concerned about issues such as dignity, respect and self-esteem.

Management experts and psychologists have shown that a salary increase isn't necessarily the ultimate motivator. Unless you can't live on your present salary, more money doesn't always inspire you. Most people work every day not just to earn money to live on, but also to satisfy their need for structure and predictability. Look at the endless number of rich people who continue to work every day.

Precisely because their basic needs are being met, today's workers don't automatically accept authoritarian styles of management. Workers' priorities have changed. Statistics show that benefits such as interesting work, sufficient help, equipment and information to get the job done and enough authority/independence to do the job mean as much to workers as good pay. None of these newly demanded benefits has anything to do with money. Each one comes from the need for self-esteem. As a manager, you should recognize that these attitudes exist. When you can delegate with the intent of increasing self-esteem in your employees, your employees will be more receptive.

> *"The only real security in this world is a reserve of knowledge, experience and ability."*
>
> *— Henry Ford*

**EXERCISE**

## Motivation Self-Assessment Worksheet

For each column, rate the most important item 1, the second most important 2 and so on.

| | What Your People Want | What You Want |
|---|---|---|
| Interesting work | _____ | _____ |
| Job security | _____ | _____ |
| Full appreciation of work done | _____ | _____ |
| Personal loyalty of supervisor | _____ | _____ |
| High salary or wages | _____ | _____ |
| Tactful discipline | _____ | _____ |
| Feeling of being "in on things" | _____ | _____ |
| Promotion in the company | _____ | _____ |
| Good working conditions | _____ | _____ |
| Help with personal problems | _____ | _____ |

Participants in many management-training seminars have completed this exercise. Their results, which have stayed consistent, are summarized below.

## EXERCISE REVIEW

### What Workers Want

| | How Workers Rated These Items | How Managers Think Their People Rated These Items |
|---|---|---|
| Full appreciation of work done | 1 | 8 |
| Feeling of being "in on things" | 2 | 10 |
| Help with personal problems | 3 | 9 |
| Job security | 4 | 2 |
| High salary or wages | 5 | 1 |
| Interesting work | 6 | 5 |
| Promotion in the company | 7 | 3 |
| Personal loyalty of supervisor | 8 | 6 |
| Good working conditions | 9 | 4 |
| Tactful discipline | 10 | 7 |

According to the results, managers tend to think the more basic needs, such as wages and job security, are more important to their employees. In reality, workers say that being appreciated and being "in on things" mean the most to them. These benefits give them a sense of belonging and build their self-esteem. This should be a clue for you when you delegate. Think about what motivates your staff members to accept your delegation. Consider, for example, the vast difference between these two requests:

1) "The Board of Directors has ordered another regional collection analysis. I'm sorry, but you'll have to contact each county chairperson to collect their totals and compile the various regional totals by tomorrow."

2) "The Board is really enthused about the campaign totals to date. They are really interested in analyzing our progress by region. We need to have updated regional totals to distribute at the meeting tomorrow."

The first delegation request motivates, but only through fear of reprimand with an implied sense of failure. Note the authoritarian tone in words like "ordered" and "you'll have to." The second request motivates with an appeal to a sense of accomplishment and belonging to the group. Note words like "enthused," "interested" and "progress." The tone is upbeat and cooperative. Instead of "*you'll* have to," it's "*we* need to." Thinking about employee motivation before you phrase your request will greatly boost your delegation efforts.

## More on Self-Esteem

Clearly, self-esteem is extremely important in delegation. As a manager, you should keep that in mind. Your words and actions can help build or weaken self-esteem in your people. You can motivate or demotivate them every time you delegate. You can enhance self-esteem in your people or in anyone else in the following ways:

1. **Actively listen.** Be alert in conversations with your people. Identify needs they express and delegate with those needs in mind.

2. **Write down others' ideas.** Show you value the input of others. Use their ideas in formulating your delegation plans.

> *"Thinking about employee motivation before you phrase your request will greatly boost your delegation efforts."*

144

3.  **Accept others' opinions.** Two heads are better than one. Ask others what they think about tasks you plan to delegate.

4.  **Take ideas seriously.** Don't ignore what others suggest. Take time to consider their ideas. It will help you improve as a delegator.

5.  **Accept differences in others.** Look upon differences as an advantage, not a problem. Recognize differences and tailor your delegation accordingly.

6.  **Give tangible rewards.** When someone completes a delegated task successfully, show your appreciation. If it's a major accomplishment, give a medal or a plaque.

7.  **Praise the specific task.** Tell the person the job was well done and the results are very useful. You'll make the person eager to accept further delegation.

8.  **Say "You are right."** Show your agreement when someone suggests the solution. Congratulate him or her for working through the delegated task to the desired result.

9.  **Support others' actions.** Don't second-guess the approach your employees take on the delegated task. Show your confidence by supporting their actions.

10. **Recognize feelings.** Feelings are at the heart of self-esteem. Know your people well and delegate with their feelings in mind. If you're considerate, they'll welcome additional delegation.

11. **Give special assignments.** You'll boost their egos by asking them to take on special assignments. You also demonstrate your confidence in them.

12. **Ask for help.** When you delegate, you show that you need help from others. That strengthens your relationship with your employees and shows you need them to accomplish your goals.

Remember, the more you bolster your people's self-esteem, the more you motivate them to produce when you delegate a task.

> " ... *The more you bolster your people's self-esteem, the more you motivate them to produce when you delegate a task.*"

## EXERCISE

Self-esteem is defined as "a confidence and satisfaction in oneself." You know when you feel it and when you lack it. Consider your relationship with your manager. Think back over the last few months. Try to recall one specific delegation-oriented instance when your manager did or said something that significantly affected your self-esteem in a *positive* way. With that instance in mind, complete the form below.

1. Briefly describe the situation and the relevant circumstances.

2. Summarize what your manager said or did that affected your self-esteem so positively.

3. Describe your reaction to the words or action.

## EXERCISE (Continued)

As you know, managers can sometimes have a *negative* effect
on self-esteem. Again, review your delegation with your
manager during the last few months. Can you think of a
situation in which your manager's words or actions
significantly affected your self-esteem in a *negative* way? If so,
complete the following worksheet.

1. Describe the situation.

2. Summarize what your manager said or did that affected you
   so negatively.

3. Describe your reaction.

4. What could your manager have done differently to make the
   experience more positive for both of you?

5. It's not too late to discuss the matter with your manager. If you
   do, what result would you like?

> *"No man is good enough to govern another man without the other's consent."*
>
> *— Abraham Lincoln*

By reviewing situations where your manager helped or hurt your self-esteem, you'll become more sensitive to how your words or actions affect your people. When you show respect and help build their self-esteem, your people will be eager to accept your delegation. They'll want to succeed to please you and themselves. If you are callous and ignore their self-esteem, you'll destroy their enthusiasm and their desire to accept delegation. You'll also lose opportunities to help them grow and develop. Never underestimate the importance of self-esteem. You must nurture it in your people and in yourself. It's one of your keys to using delegation to develop your people.

As we discussed earlier, for you to use delegation successfully to help your people develop, you must:

1. Know your people.

2. Understand their development needs.

3. Involve them in the planning phase.

4. Identify potential delegation tasks.

5. Match the task to the need.

6. Get their commitment.

7. Monitor progress and provide feedback.

## Listen to Understand

In Chapter 1 we listed several ways for you to get to know your people better so you could delegate appropriate tasks. The first was "Talk to them!" Let's refine that further by stating it a different way:

> **Listen to them!**

Managers are often so busy talking *to* their people that they don't take time to listen. It's often a one-way process. You're sending, but you're not receiving. During the course of your career you've probably had some speech and writing training, but how many people do you know who have had formal training in *listening?* Have you?

In his book, *The Seven Habits of Highly Effective People,* Stephen Covey describes five levels of listening. The highest level is what he calls "empathic listening," listening with the intent *to understand*. Covey writes:

> "Empathic listening involves much more than registering, reflecting, or even understanding the words that are said. Communication experts estimate, in fact, that only 10 percent of our communications is represented by the words we say. Another 30 percent is represented by our sounds, and 60 percent by our body language. In empathic listening, you listen with your ears, but you also, and more importantly, listen with your eyes and with your heart. You listen for feeling, for meaning. You listen for behavior. You use your right brain as well as your left. You sense, you intuit, you feel."

(*The Seven Habits of Highly Effective People,* by Stephen Covey. Copyright 1989 by Stephen R. Covey. Reprinted by permission of Simon & Schuster.)

When trying to get to know your people better, *that's* the kind of listening to use. It will help you understand their development needs. So often we *assume* we know what people think and want without even talking with them. It's amazing what we can learn by asking questions and listening. Show your people the respect they deserve — listen to them. Listen so you can *understand*. By doing this, you'll identify delegation opportunities that will help them develop.

> *"We have two ears and one mouth that we may listen the more and talk the less."*
>
> *— Zeno*

**EXERCISE**

## Rate Yourself as a Delegator Who Listens

Put a check mark in the appropriate column for each of the following questions. Be honest with yourself.

| | Never | Sometimes | Usually |
|---|---|---|---|
| When delegating a task to another person, do you: | | | |
| 1) Listen attentively to their responses without letting your mind wander? | _____ | _____ | _____ |
| 2) Listen to the entire conversation, not just parts? | _____ | _____ | _____ |
| 3) Maintain eye contact during the entire delegation discussion? | _____ | _____ | _____ |
| 4) Pay attention to tone of voice and body language, not just words? | _____ | _____ | _____ |
| 5) Avoid interrupting the person in mid-sentence? | _____ | _____ | _____ |
| 6) Avoid distractions and calls so you won't be interrupted? | _____ | _____ | _____ |

**Give yourself a score of**

    0    for each check mark in the "Never" column

    2    for each check mark in the "Sometimes" column

    3    for each check mark in the "Usually" column

**If your score is**

    27-30    You are probably an excellent delegator and known as a listener.

    20-26    You are a good delegator who recognizes the importance of listening.

    Below 20    You need to improve your delegation skills by listening more carefully.

To delegate effectively, you must know your employees and understand their needs. Listening carefully to them will help you know them better.

### Case Study

Nancy is a young manager on the fast track. She's ambitious, hard-working and dedicated to her job. She's made it clear she wants to be the company's first woman vice president. Her first six years suggest she has potential to reach that level. As part of her development, Nancy has been appointed assistant plant manager to learn manufacturing.

The plant manager, Harold, is not excited about his new assistant. He doesn't believe women can handle the rough manufacturing environment. Nancy says she wants to develop people through delegation, and Harold's concerned she'll stir up people by delegating and disrupt the entire plant operation. However, he agrees to let her plan delegation assignments as long as he can veto her suggestions.

**C A S E   S T U D Y**

151

Two months later Nancy meets with Harold to discuss her delegation plans. She tells Harold she wants Jerry to issue the monthly production report. Harold objects because he says Jerry knows nothing about computers.

"Harold, when I arrived Jerry *didn't* know anything about computers, but he does now! I talked with him and asked him how he could contribute more significantly to the plant's operation. He said he's intrigued by computers, but never had a chance to learn them. He said if he knew how to use them he could prepare reports. We signed him up for a computer course, and he's really enthused. He says his job isn't boring, and he's anxious to get to work each day."

"Well, if he was so interested in computers, why didn't he *say* so?"

"I asked him that question. He said nobody ever asked him what he'd like to do. I've learned Jerry's rather shy and tends to keep to himself. But once you show an interest in him, he really opens up. I think he's an excellent employee who just needs more guidance and understanding. So that's my plan for Jerry."

Harold agrees with Nancy's plan for Jerry. She then tells him about Sue. She's asked Sue to give the quarterly talk to the Quality Council. Nancy's learned that Sue's an outstanding speaker who is president of the local Toastmasters Club and teaches speech in night school. Her former manager never bothered to learn about her special skills and never considered her for important speaking assignments. Sue's very enthused and pleased that Nancy is trying to help her.

Reluctantly, Harold endorses Nancy's delegation plans for Jerry and Sue. "I'm pleased, Nancy," he says, "I thought you would disrupt the plant with your delegation plans, but you've shown you understand what 'developing people through delegation' means."

## Comment

Harold was very concerned that Nancy would upset his employees by asking them to take on more responsibility. He failed to recognize their need for someone who would listen to them and work with them to improve and develop. Nancy talked with her people, learned about their interests and skills and found tasks to delegate that would strengthen the individuals and the organization. She knew the power of delegation and how to use it to develop her people.

- Did this case study bring home any particular message about delegating to you? If so, what was it?

_____

_____

_____

_____

## Summary

Delegation can be a very powerful way to develop your people, but to do it well takes effort and practice. You must know your people and understand their needs. You must also know the task you want to delegate so you can match the task and the employee for an optimum delegation experience.

Remember, create a climate that fosters growth and development. If you have that climate and delegate wisely within it, you, your employees and the entire organization will benefit.

> "*A manager ... sets objectives ... organizes ... motivates and communicates ... measure[s] ... [and] develops people. Every manager does these things — knowingly or not. A manager may do them well, or may do them wretchedly, but always does them.*"
>
> — *Peter Drucker*

153

## QUESTIONS FOR PERSONAL DEVELOPMENT

1. What is the major emphasis of this chapter?

2. What do you feel are the most important things you learned from this chapter?

   1)

   2)

   3)

3. How can you apply what you learned to your current job?

   1)

   2)

   3)

4. What objectives will you set for improvement? By when (date)?

   **Objective:**                              **By When?**

   1)

   2)

   3)

5. Who can help you most in applying what you learned in this chapter?

6. What are the major roadblocks that might hinder your progress in applying what you learned in this chapter?

    **Roadblock:**                  **Why?**

1)

2)

3)

7. How will you communicate the most important points in this chapter to others in your organization?

8. What preparation is necessary to introduce better delegation?

9. What changes do you expect to make that will better motivate your team?

      **Change:**               **By when?**

1)

2)

3)

10. How will you monitor your progress to assure that performance has improved or productivity has increased? (reports, meetings, etc.)

11. What work-related problems concern you most in evaluating how you will benefit from this chapter?

12. What changes do you expect to see in yourself one year from now as a result of what you learned in this chapter?

# *C* *HAPTER 7*

# The Delegation Conference

A recurrent theme of effective delegation is "Take time up front to avoid wasting time later." Or "Explain now and you won't have to complain later." Nowhere do these warnings mean more than when you conduct the delegation conference.

Some managers approach delegation with good intentions and a well-conceived plan. They analyze their jobs, pick appropriate tasks to delegate, set realistic goals and match the tasks with the right employees. Then they destroy the benefit of all that careful preparation by flubbing the next step. When it's crucial to spend meaningful time in the delegation conference with the employee, they rush through the discussion and send the employee away confused and poorly informed. After doing so much so well, they set the stage for failure by giving scant attention to the delegation conference.

Don't delegate on the run. A hallway or noisy meeting is not the place to pass along information required for an important delegation. Schedule sufficient time, without interruption, in your office for the delegation conference. You want to allow enough time for discussion and questions. A major assignment may require an hour, a simple task only 15 or 20 minutes. But don't rush the discussion. You want to cover all the steps.

The first step in delegation is planning the conference. You must give some thought to the delegation process before the

> *"Any fool can criticize, condemn, and complain — and most fools do."*
>
> *— Dale Carnegie*

actual conference. Know what supplies, resources and authority the employee will need to do the work. Anticipate what questions or problems the employee might have. Commit to paper your goals for the work. Once you're ready for the delegation conference, follow these six specific steps for delegating work to someone.

## The Six Steps in the Delegation Process

1. **State the desired results.** Explain the results you want the person to achieve. Don't start with the actual tasks required to do the work. Start with the results you want achieved. Don't stress methods over results. That limits your employee and weakens the impact of your delegation. You may be surprised at your employee's creativity in devising ways to reach the desired results. The goal is mutual agreement on an objective achievement.

   Consider the difference between these two delegations:

   a) "Katie, make 500 copies of these personnel changes on company letterhead and send one to every store manager. Get on it right away."

   b) "Katie, there are 500 store managers in the chain, and I need to let all of them know about these personnel changes as soon as possible. I'd like you to handle it. Would you give it some thought and discuss it with me in half an hour?"

   Katie may surprise you by suggesting she include the memo in the avidly read company newsletter, which is about to go to press. Or she may say that the only way to do it is to send out 500 form letters. She may also surprise you by not having the vaguest idea of what to do. Great! You now have the chance to teach Katie two things. There are several ways to spread information to 500 people, and you rely on her ideas as well as her help and will keep asking for both as you delegate.

*"Never tell people how to do things. Tell them what to do and they will surprise you with their ingenuity."*

*— George S. Patton*

2. **Commit the goals to paper.** When you agree on the goals, write them down. State the goal of the project and the performance standard that will measure it in 20 words or less. If it takes longer than this, rethink the delegation and break it into smaller, more specific functions. Train your people and yourself to review these goals periodically. If it's a short task, one or two brief reviews may be adequate. A six-month project may require a monthly review to be sure the goals are still appropriate. Reviewing the goals will avoid confusion on all sides.

3. **Establish a time line.** If the employee doesn't think he can meet your suggested deadline, be flexible when possible and work out a more suitable time limit. Allowing the person to set his own deadline is far preferable to forcing yours upon him. He'll feel greater ownership of the task if he can help set the deadline.

   However, circumstances may sometimes dictate that you set the deadline. Make sure the employee knows what priority the delegated task should take. Realize that not everything you delegate can "take precedence." This does nothing except frustrate. Do you really want him to "drop everything" to take on this project? Specific deadlines are a must. Avoid indefinite deadlines such as "whenever you can get to it" or "by sometime next month." Be sure to establish some kind of reporting process so you can keep abreast of progress. Together, schedule the necessary reviews. Doing this together gives the employee a chance to consider other workload demands on his time. For a simple task, one or two reviews may be sufficient; more complex tasks require regular meetings with specific agendas and mini-deadlines. Make sure the person knows that all review times and the final deadline are firm.

4. **Grant the necessary authority.** Whenever you assign work, you must give the person power to act and to exercise initiative. Make sure that all people affected by the delegation know that you've delegated authority to this person. If appropriate, introduce your employee to everyone helping to

complete the task, including supervisors, co-workers and support staff. Make it clear that your person now has authority to do the job and that you expect him or her to work through any problems that arise.

5. **Assign responsibility/accountability.** Always delegate an entire task. This heightens the employee's interest and sense of accomplishment. Granting authority makes your delegation more effective. Stress your confidence in the employee at every opportunity, even if you have to force yourself. Don't show fake confidence, but do compliment the employee throughout the task when something is done well. Your support often means more than your specific advice. Review work only at scheduled times or when the job is finished.

   Stressing the delegatee's accountability for the entire task accomplishes two things. First, it makes clear that the ball is in the employee's court. The employee carries the responsibility for results. Of course, you're still ultimately responsible to your own manager, but your employee is accountable to you. You can leave no room for confusion about that. Second, accountability adds to the employee's sense of independence. It provides positive pressure and motivation to perform. Emphasize that the employee is free to make decisions relevant to the assigned task. To some employees, this may be a new experience. Make it clear that, within certain limits, what they decide in this matter goes. Be sure they understand what those limits are. Don't make them guess.

6. **Get acceptance of the project.** Always make sure your person gives you clear and definite acceptance of the delegated task and a commitment to follow through. You want more than murmured approval or tacit acceptance. You need an outright statement that the person agrees on the goals and the deadline. Perhaps you should both sign copies of the revised statement of goals and time lines.

> *"The surest way to corrupt a young man is to teach him to esteem more highly those who think alike than those who think differently."*
>
> *— Friedrich Nietzsche*

You might use a simple written format like this:

| | |
|---|---|
| **We met** | _____(date)_____ |
| **We discussed** | _____(delegation topic)_____ |
| **We agreed on Goal:** | _____ |
| **Deadline:** | _____(date)_____ |

**Signed** _____  **Signed** _____

    **Employee**                           **Manager**

When you see all you must accomplish in a delegation conference, you can understand why it takes time to conduct one properly. The conference really sets the foundation for the employee to proceed. When the employee leaves the conference, he should have a *clear understanding* of:

1) The desired results.

2) The time line.

3) The authority he has to achieve the results.

4) His accountability.

5) How results will be measured.

> *"I make it a rule only to believe what I understand."*
>
> — *Benjamin Disraeli*

> *"No man really becomes a fool until he stops asking questions."*
>
> *— Charles Steinmetz*

It takes time to cover all these points, but it's time well spent. If you approach delegation of a task in a sloppy or haphazard way, you tell your employee that the task isn't very important, even though it may be. On the other hand, if you conduct a thorough, well-organized delegation conference, you send a clear message that the task has high priority with you. Your employee will likely respond favorably and tackle the assignment with enthusiasm.

Remember, we're discussing the delegation *conference*. Don't approach it as just a session where you pass out assignments. Seek input from your people. Ask for ideas, comments, suggestions and questions. You'll have a more productive conference, and the employee will feel more committed to the outcome.

## EXERCISE

Think about the last task or activity your manager delegated to you. Describe it in a few words and then answer the following questions.

**Task/Activity:** _____

_____

1. *Where* did the actual act of delegation take place (your manager's office, your office, hallway, cafeteria, etc.)?

_____

|  |  | YES | NO |
|---|---|---|---|
| 2. | Did your manager clearly define what results he wanted? | — | — |
| 3. | Did your manager avoid telling you *how to* achieve the results? | — | — |
| 4. | Did your manager establish a definite deadline for accomplishing the task? | — | — |
| 5. | Did your manager set any intermediate reviews to monitor progress? | — | — |
| 6. | Did your manager give you the authority necessary to accomplish the task? | — | — |
| 7. | Did your manager set clear limits to your delegated authority? | — | — |
| 8. | Did your manager make it clear you would be held accountable for achieving the results? | — | — |

## EXERCISE (Continued)

|  | YES | NO |
|---|---|---|
| 9. Did your manager obtain your acceptance of the project and commitment to achieve the results? | ___ | ___ |
| 10. Did your manager seek your ideas, comments, suggestions and questions? | ___ | ___ |
| 11. Were you satisfied when you left the meeting that you had the necessary information and authority to proceed with the task? | ___ | ___ |
| 12. Would you describe the meeting with your manager as truly a "delegation conference"? | ___ | ___ |
| 13. Did (or will) the delegated task contribute to your development? | ___ | ___ |

If you answered "yes" to most of the questions, your manager takes delegation seriously and tries to establish a firm base for you to begin a delegated task. You're fortunate to report to such an excellent delegator.

If you answered "no" to most of the questions, skillful delegation may not be a high priority with your manager. Talk with him and tell him you value the experience you get from delegation, but you'd be more effective if he'd help you set goals, establish firm deadlines and provide follow-up. Try to help him become a better delegator, but be tactful.

Note the exercise asked only about the *last* task your manager delegated to you. Obviously, to judge your manager as a delegator, you should consider whether your last delegation experience was typical.

You can, of course, use the exercise to rate your own delegation practices. Think about how you handled the act of delegation in the past. Did you hold true delegation conferences with your people? Review the questions and rate yourself. Or better yet, give the exercise to your people and ask them to rate you. Don't be discouraged if your rating is low. Just resolve to improve, using what you've learned. And remember, devoting enough time to your people in the delegation conference will almost certainly save both of you time later.

## Accountability in Delegation

Accountability as it relates to delegation often causes confusion. Let's see why.

### Case Study

David is the new finance director of a computer software company. Patricia, the president, delegates responsibility to him for filing the corporate income tax return by April 15. She tells him: "How you want to accomplish the task is up to you, but *you are accountable for the results.*"

Steve is a supervisor who reports to David. To get help with the task and also give Steve valuable experience, David asks him to assemble all the expense data from the previous year that's needed to file the tax return. David tells Steve: "I trust you, so I won't hound you. Just get the expense data to me by March 15."

For two months David works on other matters, ignoring the tax return. On March 15 he contacts Steve to collect the expense data. Steve tells him he doesn't have the data because marketing hasn't provided its input. David's very upset. He knows he'll never make the filing deadline.

> *"Tact is the art of making a point without making an enemy."*
>
> *— Howard W. Newton*

**CASE STUDY**

"Why didn't you tell me you were having problems, Steve?"

"You said you wouldn't hound me, so I didn't think you wanted *me* to bother *you* either," answered Steve.

David calls Patricia to break the news to her. "Our tax return will be late, and we'll have to pay a penalty. I delegated part of the job to Steve, and he screwed up. I gave him responsibility for one small part of the job, and he failed to deliver. I took care of *my* responsibilities, but he muffed his."

**Analysis**

Patricia was not pleased with David's performance. During her discussion with him, she learned the following:

- David had held a comprehensive delegation conference with Steve, but never monitored Steve's progress on the delegated task.

- David accused Steve of muffing his responsibilities, but David claimed he took care of his own.

- David thought he could delegate a task and abdicate responsibility for it.

When you delegate, remember:

- Hold a comprehensive delegation conference.

- Monitor your employee's progress toward completion of the task.

- You can delegate a task, but you can't abdicate responsibility for what you delegate.

- Support your people, and don't abandon them when you should stick by them.

*"You can delegate a task, but you can't abdicate responsibility for what you delegate."*

166

## Questions

- If you were David, what would you have done differently in the delegation conference with Steve?

  _____

  _____

  _____

  _____

- How do you think David conducted himself when he informed Patricia of the delay?

  _____

  _____

  _____

  _____

- If you were Steve, what could you have said or done during the delegation conference that might have helped you avoid the unfortunate results?

  _____

  _____

  _____

  _____

- What should Steve have done when he first suspected he might have trouble meeting his deadline?

  _____

  _____

  _____

  _____

## Delegation and the Organization's Goals

Contrary to what some believe, most people really *do* want to contribute in their jobs. They don't put in time just for the paycheck. They want to feel that their efforts help move the organization toward its goals. That gives them pride and a sense of accomplishment.

As a manager, recognize this desire by explaining how the task you're delegating relates to your organization's goals. It should take only a few minutes, but it can be a powerful motivator.

Consider the contrast in these two delegations.

a) "Ed, I'm asking you to take responsibility for specifying and ordering two new blending mixers for our premium paint line. They have to be up and running by July 1. They are absolutely necessary for us to meet our goal of increasing production by 10 percent this year. The money to purchase them is already authorized. Joe is available to help you whenever you need him. Your success with this task will ensure we meet our production goal. Keep me advised of your progress."

b) "Ed, I'm pretty busy this month, so I want you to specify and order two new blending mixers that we need. We probably should have them by July 1. The money's available, so don't worry about that. Let me know when they're installed."

Which approach clearly relates the task to the organization's goals?

Taking time to explain to your people the importance of the task you're delegating and how it relates to your organization's goals is well worth the effort. It accomplishes several things.

1. It reminds your people of the organization's goals and strengthens their importance.

2. It shows that you're goal-oriented and that you want your people to be also.

3. It helps you and your people focus on high-priority matters, such as those that further your goals.

4. It serves as a reminder to identify activities that *don't* further your goals and to get rid of them.

5. It forces you to make sure *you* understand and can clearly communicate your organization's goals.

If you can't explain how the task you plan to delegate relates to the organization's goals, you should reconsider whether that task should be done at all by *anyone*.

> *"Taking time to explain the importance of a task you're delegating forces you to make sure you understand and can clearly communicate your organization's goals."*

## EXERCISE

Test how well you relate delegated tasks to your organization's "big picture." Recall the last time you delegated a task to one of your people and answer the following questions.

### Task

- What was the task?

  _____

  _____

- How did it relate to the organization's goals?

  _____

  _____

  _____

- Did you explain the relationship when you delegated the task?

  _____

  _____

- If not, could you explain it today?

  _____

  _____

Again, don't be discouraged if you haven't been discussing organizational goals when you delegate. Many managers don't. It takes only a few extra minutes, but it can improve the delegation conference and its impact on the employee significantly. It should also boost your overall skill as a delegator. So give it a try next time you delegate.

## A Further Look at Responsibility

In the previous case study, David thought he could avoid responsibility by delegating. That's a myth. Managers who delegate have broad shoulders. They must accept complete responsibility if their delegation is less than successful. Assigning duties to others is not a passport to freedom from worry and responsibility. That escape hatch is abdication, not delegation. Ultimate accountability rests permanently with the person who delegates. Problems inherent in delegation tie directly to the emotions of those involved. The delegator must think through how he'll act if he discovers that an assigned task has gone off track. He must realize that actions others take may differ from those he would have taken, and he must accept those differences.

Accommodation of differences is perhaps the hardest part of learning to delegate. While it's easy to accept the idea that people are not the same, it's much harder to act accordingly. You may find immense variations not only in the *quality* and *quantity* of the work your employees perform, but also in the *ways* they perform the work. The manager must be prepared to live with his people's methods and decisions. It's a big order, but you can't reap the benefits of delegation unless you're willing to accept the risks. You don't have to agree with your people at all times, but you must never leave them hanging out to dry. Your people depend on you. If you don't support them when they need you, you'll lose their trust in your leadership. (Remember how David "supported" Steve?)

*"Failing organizations are usually over-managed and under-led."*

*— Warren G. Bennis*

171

## Delegation Takes Courage

You need courage to risk delegating. Managers typically avoid taking chances, but delegation is a calculated risk, and you must expect that over time the gains will surpass the losses. You must recognize the risk and adjust emotionally and intellectually in order to delegate effectively.

Delegation is risky because you're never *absolutely* sure of the outcome of a task you delegate. You may lose control. The task may not be completed satisfactorily. You may have to take the blame for an occasional failure. But remember, when you delegate you free up valuable time. You develop your people. You strengthen the entire organization. These gains will surely overshadow the occasional delegation that fails to meet your expectations.

Give your people credit for their successes with delegated tasks. Congratulate them publicly. Write them notes of appreciation. Mention their accomplishments to your management. But if they fail, take the blame yourself. Demonstrate your support for them. Sound unfair? It is, but it's an important and necessary rule to follow when delegating. The key word is trust. To build a team, your people must have confidence that you'll always be there for them.

Why should your people knock themselves out for you if you're going to bask in the glory of their work? Teamwork is essential, but the coach must credit his players, not polish his own star. The delegator does need broad shoulders, but also a small enough ego to leave the spotlight to the people who did the work.

## Summary

President Harry Truman had a sign on his desk, "The Buck Stops Here." He understood delegation and responsibility. He knew that ultimate accountability rests with the person at the top. How well do you support your people? Do you ever hang them out to dry?

Many things can go wrong when you delegate. However, if you hold a thorough delegation conference, you can greatly reduce the chance that problems will develop. Take the time to plan a comprehensive delegation conference. It's worth it.

*"Reading maketh a full man, conference a ready man..."*

*— Francis Bacon*

## QUESTIONS FOR PERSONAL DEVELOPMENT

1. What is the major emphasis of this chapter?

2. What do you feel are the most important things you learned from this chapter?

   1)

   2)

   3)

3. How can you apply what you learned to your current job?

   1)

   2)

   3)

4. What objectives will you set for improvement? By when (date)?

   **Objective:**                    **By When?**

   1)

   2)

   3)

5. Who can help you most in applying what you learned in this chapter?

6. What are the major roadblocks that might hinder your progress in applying what you learned in this chapter?

   **Roadblock:**                    **Why?**

   1)

   2)

   3)

7. How will you communicate the most important points in this chapter to others in your organization?

8. What preparation is necessary to introduce better delegation?

9. What changes do you expect to make that will better motivate your team?

**Change:**               **By when?**

1)

2)

3)

10. How will you monitor to assure that performance has improved or productivity has increased? (reports, meetings, etc.)

11. What work-related problems concern you most in evaluating how you will benefit from this chapter?

12. What changes do you expect to see in yourself one year from now as a result of what you learned in this chapter?

## CHAPTER 8

# Let Go ... But Follow Up

Once you've delegated a task, let your employee have a fair try at it. Don't meddle! Let the employee do it, even if it's not "the right way." Avoid trespassing on authority once you give it. Make sure the jobs you give your people are whole and important, and make sure you really *give* them the jobs. Delegation, like a kite, won't fly unless you give it enough slack to soar. If you take back or short-circuit assignments, your interference will only frustrate your employees, and they'll be less likely to do the task well.

## Learning from Mistakes

Helping an employee grow and improve by devising a series of successes doesn't mean seeking to avoid all mistakes when you delegate. Not every delegated task gets done correctly. In fact, mistakes are a key part of learning through experience. Mistakes show what not to do. And the person who has learned what not to do is wiser than the person who's never been allowed to venture far enough to make an error. Of course, you don't want your employees to make so many errors that they get intimidated, so you limit the chances for mistakes.

Remember, an employee's failure to do an assigned task right may simply mean you're delegating without following through. Your controls may have failed. If a person doesn't

> *"Once you've delegated a task, let your employee have a fair try at it. Don't meddle!"*

complete a task, take another look at the goals. Are they stated clearly? Are they realistic? Are you monitoring progress toward the goals? Proper systems for monitoring employees' work should prevent large-scale failures.

Once employees recognize they've made errors, don't rub it in. Stress the positive. Find something they did right and compliment them. Then correct their mistakes and show how they might have avoided them. For example, suppose your truck driver delivers a rush order to your most important customer before the deadline and then wrecks his pickup speeding back to the plant. Congratulate him for keeping the customer happy, but talk to him about his driving habits. Remember, reprimand only when the person can do better. When you leave your people after a reprimand, you want them to think about what they did wrong, not the way you treated them. Allow yourself only a few minutes to share your feelings. When it's over, it's over. Don't keep beating up the person for the same mistake.

In the same way, focus on efforts, not circumstances. When you end a reprimand with praise, people think about their behavior, not yours. People can take only a limited amount of criticism at any one time. When they reach their limit, they get defensive, start to reject the validity of the criticism and "tune out" altogether. So when someone really bungles an assignment, try to help him or her iron out the wrinkles gradually rather than dumping all the bad news at one time. And mix in a little praise with the bitter medicine to help the person swallow it.

## Follow-Up

You need to let go and give your employee breathing room when you delegate. It demonstrates your confidence and helps build confidence in your employee. But you *must* follow up to make sure the delegated task stays on track.

Remember David and Steve in the last chapter? David let go completely! He arranged no mini-deadlines or reviews to monitor Steve's progress in assembling the necessary data for the company's income tax return. He may have thought he was showing great confidence in Steve, but he didn't use good judgment. He failed to monitor Steve's progress toward the

---

*"There is no failure except in no longer trying."*

*— Elbert Hubbard*

---

*"The best executive is the one who has sense enough to pick good men to do what he wants done, and self-restraint enough to keep from meddling with them while they do it."*

*— Theodore Roosevelt*

goal. Had he done so, Steve's problems could have been avoided.

David's remarks to Patricia also showed he thought he'd delegated *total* responsibility for Steve's part of the project. He tried to chuck responsibility.

Never forget that what you were responsible for before delegating, you are responsible for after delegating. Follow-up is key to the delegation process. Finding the right degree of follow-up — guiding without meddling, protecting against disaster without pampering, advising without reducing accountability — is a complicated, subtle aspect of the art of delegation. To avoid letting a delegated task get away from you, set up automatic system checks so you'll get regular "flash reports" (weekly, daily, monthly or whatever is appropriate) on how it's coming. New data from these reports may lead you to readjust the project. Or you may find the project in chaos, at which time you can get involved and get it back on track. The best way to get a surprise in business is to delegate a project and then forget about it until it's due. And in business, surprises are rarely good.

## Spot-Checking — An Example

Cynthia, an assistant editor at the Daily Tribune, believes in delegating authority just as the management books tell her to. A very busy woman, she wants desperately to unload some responsibility on her staff. Here's what happened to copy that almost missed print in a special section because another editor let some preliminary story deadlines slide by.

Richard, the special project coordinator, was furious because the featured articles on local medical specialists had not yet been written. He did not want to print the section as it had been the previous year, using wire-supplied copy. Cynthia knew the deadline would be tight when she promised Richard that she would meet it.

Cynthia immediately pulled together the list of stories and sources for the special section. She personally placed the list on Doug's desk with a big note written in red stating, "Doug,

**Example**

get on this right away. Very hot deadline!" How was she to know that Doug, her best medical reporter, would be out for a week because of a family emergency?

Two weeks later, when Cynthia was on her way to an editor's meeting, she saw Doug and asked how the project was progressing. When Doug looked confused, Cynthia sensed trouble. When she specified which special section, Doug said, "Oh, that one. I did not see your note until three days ago when I got back from the funeral. By the way, there are a few things I need you to verify before I go on. The main story about Dr. Nixon is going to be difficult to complete because he is out of town until next month. So, is there another source you want me to contact for that story or do you want me to focus on another medical specialty?" Cynthia was angry with Doug and berated him in the newsroom in front of the other reporters, which she knew she shouldn't do. The problem was that Cynthia was more angry at herself for not having the good sense to check on the project sooner.

That's what happens to people who hope for the best and don't get it.

You can monitor delegation in many ways: oral conferences, written summaries, formal reports, flowcharts, checklists, calendars, etc. The key factor here is that you must have a time line. You must control to avoid disaster. The responsibility rests with you.

Letting go and following up are related concepts. The key is to find the right balance. You need to consider the capability of your employee, as well as the complexity and importance of the delegated task. If you let go completely, you won't follow up at all. If you refuse to let go even slightly, you'll be pestering your employee constantly with questions about project status. You should avoid both extremes.

*"When you have a supervisor checking a man on a job, he's not a supervisor. He's a checker."*

*— Frederick Herzberg*

## EXERCISE

Consider your own style of delegating and reflect on the previous remarks about responsibility, letting go and follow-up. Recall an instance in recent weeks when you delegated a task to an employee and answer the following questions.

- Task/Activity delegated:

  _____

  _____

- Employee: _____

- Did you delegate the task or activity for (check all that apply):

  Direct results?        _____

  Development?        _____

  Evaluation?        _____

- Did you conduct a "delegation conference" with your employee?

  _____

## EXERCISE (Continued)

|  | YES | NO |
|---|---|---|

- If so, did you:

    1) State the desired results clearly? ___ ___

    2) Establish a time line? ___ ___

    3) Grant the necessary authority? ___ ___

    4) Assign responsibility/accountability? ___ ___

    5) Get acceptance of the project? ___ ___

    6) Relate the project to the goals of the
       organization? ___ ___

    7) Seek input from your employee during
       the conference? ___ ___

- When you established the time line, did you
  indicate the means you would use to monitor
  the delegation? ___ ___

- Did you set definite times for progress reports? ___ ___

## EXERCISE (Continued)

- Check the means you said would be used for progress reports:

    _____ Oral conferences
    _____ Written summaries
    _____ Formal reports
    _____ Flowcharts
    _____ Checklists
    _____ Calendars
    _____ Other

- If the project you delegated is still under way, how is it progressing? (If it's finished, answer the questions accordingly.)

    _____

    _____

    _____

- Are you monitoring it as you said you would? _____

    If not, why not?_____

    _____

- Do you expect it to be finished by the deadline? _____

## EXERCISE (Continued)

- Have new developments forced you to make any changes in your original plan?

  _____

  _____

  _____

- Based on what you've seen so far, what would you do differently?

  _____

  _____

  _____

- Overall, do you expect this to be a successful delegation experience? Explain.

  _____

  _____

  _____

## Analyze and Improve

If you're like most managers, you probably never tried to analyze your delegation style thoroughly. You just delegated without giving it much thought. Most of your attempts were pretty successful, so it never occurred to you to examine them. But why settle for "pretty successful"? If you look closely at your delegation practices, identify your weak points and take steps to correct them, you can steadily improve your skills. As your skills get better, so should your results. You'll move from pretty successful to very successful. You'll accomplish more through your people, and they'll learn and develop. Your entire organization will benefit. So take time to review past delegation experiences. It should help you do better in the future.

## The Right Degree of Follow-Up

When you decide how closely to monitor a delegated task, keep four things in mind:

1. The complexity and importance of the task

2. The consequences of failing to meet the deadline

3. The capability of the employee

4. The morale and development of the employee

Ignoring any one of these could cause problems or at least cut the overall impact of the delegation. You should weigh them all to decide how closely you need to monitor a given delegation.

Let's consider some examples.

"If you ride a horse, sit close and tight. If you ride a man, sit easy and light."

— *Benjamin Franklin*

**Example**

### Example #1

John is chief pilot of the corporate aircraft fleet. One of his duties is to train recently hired pilots in the new jet the company just bought. He and Ernie, one of the new pilots, are on a training flight. To familiarize Ernie with the controls, John delegates different tasks to him to see how he responds. As they head west at 10,000 feet, they cross the Kansas-Colorado border. John tells Ernie, "At exactly 0900 hours, take her up in a steep climb to 24,000 feet. Then level off. I think we should try to go *over* the Rockies rather than *through* them."

John has stated the task for Ernie very clearly:
Take the plane up in a steep climb [action verb]
to 24,000 feet [measurable result] at 0900 hours
[time to accomplish objective].

Being a conscientious delegator, John wants to monitor the task at just the right level. So he reviews the following checklist in his head:

1. How complex or important is the task?
   (For an experienced pilot, making a steep climb is easy. Nothing complex to worry about. However, it is important.)

2. What are the consequences of failing to meet the deadline?
   (If Ernie is five minutes late starting his climb, we're history!)

3. How capable is the employee?
   (Ernie is a good pilot with relevant experience.)

4. How will monitoring affect the employee's morale and development?
   (Ernie is very proud of his flying ability. If I watch him too closely, he'll get upset.)

## Example #2

Karen, a marketing supervisor for a food-processing company, is responsible for conducting a consumer survey to assess acceptability of a new low-fat chocolate cake. Roger is a co-op student working in Karen's group for the summer. She's decided to ask Roger to conduct the consumer survey. It would be good experience for him. Results of the survey must be ready by October 1.

On June 15, Karen meets with Roger in her office to discuss the delegation with him. Even though he's only a student, she describes the task and conducts a complete delegation conference because it will help Roger get off to the right start. They agree he'll interview 50 consumers to determine their opinions of the new chocolate cake and write a summary report by September 1. As Roger leaves Karen's office, he says, "Karen, one thing you didn't mention — how will you monitor my progress on this job?" She replies, "I'll get back to you tomorrow on that, Roger."

Karen decides on her follow-up plan and creates the following chart to summarize it:

Example

## Delegation Follow-Up Plan

**Task:** Consumer Survey     **Employee:** Roger
**Date Delegated:** June 15     **Date Due:** September 1

| Date | Follow-Up Required | Suggested Method |
|------|--------------------|------------------|
| June 20 | Review schedule Roger develops | Oral conference with flowchart |
| July 10 | Review draft of questionnaire | Written summary |
| July 20 | All interviewees contacted? | Oral conference |
| Aug. 10 | Interviews completed? | Oral conference |
| Aug. 20 | Review draft of final report | Written summary |

As soon as she finishes the chart, she gives Roger a copy so they are both working toward the same follow-up schedule.

## EXERCISE

Consider a task you plan to delegate to an employee during the next month. Try to imagine the main steps that must be taken to complete it. Choose an employee and a due date. Then consider:

1.  The complexity and importance of the task

2.  The consequences of failing to meet the deadline

3.  The capability of the employee you selected

4.  The morale and development of the employee

Using the information you develop, design a Delegation Follow-Up Plan patterned after Karen's approach and complete the chart below.

---

### Delegation Follow-Up Plan

Task: _____   Delegatee: _____

Date Delegated: _____   Date Due: _____

| Date | Follow-Up Required | Suggested Method |
|------|--------------------|------------------|
| _____ | _____ | _____ |
| _____ | _____ | _____ |
| _____ | _____ | _____ |
| _____ | _____ | _____ |
| _____ | _____ | _____ |
| _____ | _____ | _____ |
| _____ | _____ | _____ |

*"The fellow who never makes a mistake takes his orders from one who does."*

*— Herbert V. Prochnow*

**C A S E  S T U D Y**

Remember, don't watch your employees too closely as they work on delegated tasks. The purpose of delegation is *not* to avoid all mistakes unless the nature of the task *demands* an error-free process. The purpose is to accomplish the desired results while giving opportunities for development. If you constantly look over your employee's shoulder, you'll cause resentment and frustration. You'll probably also stifle creativity and imagination, which can blossom in the right delegation environment. Too much follow-up can ruin a delegation experience that has been well-conceived and well-initiated. Be sensitive to that possibility and guard against overzealous monitoring.

Once again, it's important to know your people well. Some may require close supervision and follow-up. Others may be extremely competent and reliable. Don't establish the same follow-up plan for the 20-year veteran who's successfully completed countless delegation tasks as you do for the inexperienced new employee who's never worked independently. Recognize the individuality of your people and build on it.

### Case Study

Wade is a manufacturing manager who's mastered the art of delegation. As a supervisor, he learned the importance of delegation and knows how to use it effectively. Apparently Wade delegates *everything.* He seldom works beyond 5 p.m. and never carries work home at night. He's never ruffled by problems at the plants because his staff handles them. He decided long ago to delegate as much as possible so he could focus on his real interest — long-range planning. Wade's boss says about him: "He gets results, meets his goals and is one of the company's best planners and thinkers."

When asked the secret of his delegation successes, Wade says, "I have no secrets. I use standard approaches to delegation, but I *insist* on appropriate follow-up. That makes or breaks delegation. For example, let me tell you about Art.

"He manages the Akron plant. He used to call me every day because his former boss demanded such feedback. I told him I trusted his judgment and just wanted him to call every Monday and give me a 10-minute status report.

He's an excellent manager and that follow-up arrangement works fine.

"Last month I asked Art to chair a committee to recommend equipment we should buy for the plant. The report's due in six months. Since I know Art's capabilities, I've asked for a one-page status report every month. If I have questions, I'll contact him. I know Art well, and I'm sure my follow-up plan is right. The keys to follow-up are to know your people, understand what's involved in the tasks you delegate and draw on your experience. If you ignore follow-up when you delegate, you invite disaster."

## Comment

Wade has major manufacturing responsibilities, but uses delegation to strengthen his staff and give himself more time for planning. He knows that successful delegation requires appropriate follow-up. Remember his belief.

The keys to follow-up are:

- Know your people

- Understand what's involved in the delegated task

- Draw on your experience

What points made in the case study will help you improve your own delegating?

Thinking about your past delegation experiences, have you considered follow-up adequately?

As a result of what you've learned about letting go and following up, what changes will you make in your own delegation practices?

> *"The man who delegates responsibilities for running the company, without knowing the intimate details of what is involved, runs the enormous risk of rendering himself superfluous."*
>
> *— Harold Geneen*

## Summary

Managers who are great at planning and conducting comprehensive delegation conferences often fail to achieve results because they bungle follow-up. To improve your odds for success, remember to establish the right follow-up plan by considering:

1. The complexity and importance of the task

2. The consequences of failing to meet the deadline

3. The capability of the employee

4. The morale and development of the employee

Choosing the right degree of follow-up isn't easy, but with practice you'll improve. Remember to maintain the right balance between totally letting go and constantly pestering the employee. Avoid those extremes. The skill with which you handle follow-up can make the difference between being a good delegator and a great one.

*"I never had a boss that tried to sit on me, and I think that's essential. If you expect people to develop, you have to give them the responsibility, you have to tell them what their objectives are and you have to let them do it."*

*— David M. Rodman*

## QUESTIONS FOR PERSONAL DEVELOPMENT

1. What is the major emphasis of this chapter?

2. What do you feel are the most important things you learned from this chapter?

   1)

   2)

   3)

3. How can you apply what you learned to your current job?

   1)

   2)

   3)

4. What objectives will you set for improvement? By when (date)?

   | **Objective:** | **By When?** |
   |----------------|--------------|
   | 1)             |              |
   | 2)             |              |
   | 3)             |              |

5. Who can help you most in applying what you learned in this chapter?

6. What are the major roadblocks that might hinder your progress in applying what you learned in this chapter?

| **Roadblock:** | **Why?** |
| --- | --- |
| 1) | |
| 2) | |
| 3) | |

7. How will you communicate the most important points in this chapter to others in your organization?

8. What preparation is necessary to introduce better delegation?

9. What changes do you expect to make that will better motivate your team?

| **Change:** | **By when?** |
| --- | --- |
| 1) | |
| 2) | |
| 3) | |

10. How will you monitor your progress to assure that performance has improved or productivity has increased? (reports, meetings, etc.)

11. What work-related problems concern you most in evaluating how you will benefit from this chapter?

12. What changes do you expect to see in yourself one year from now as a result of what you learned in this chapter?

# *C* HAPTER 9

# Feedback and Criticism in Delegation

Follow-up is essential to successful delegation. You can't delegate a task, ignore its progress and expect to reap the full benefits of the delegation. You need to work with your employees to establish a follow-up plan every time you delegate. The plan may involve only one or two brief conversations during the course of a simple task. Or it may require extensive progress reports while your employee works on a six-month project. It's your responsibility to set the right level of follow-up for the task. But in every case, make sure you follow up.

Earlier we discussed the importance of finding the right degree of follow-up. You want to guide your employee without interfering, protect against disaster without pampering and advise without diminishing accountability. Finding the right degree of follow-up is an art. If you know your people well and understand the tasks you delegate, you can judge the right level of follow-up for each task.

Follow-up of a delegated task includes two important responsibilities for the delegator. You must:

1.  Monitor progress of the task.

2.  Give your employee feedback.

> *" ... Establish a follow-up plan every time you delegate."*

In the last chapter we discussed the first responsibility, monitoring progress of the task. Now let's focus on feedback.

## The Importance of Feedback

Some managers are very diligent about checking on a delegated task's progress. They ask questions, request reports and stay informed about what's happening. They collect information so *they'll* know what's going on. They take the first responsibility of follow-up very seriously — monitoring progress of the task. But they don't follow through on the second responsibility — giving your employee feedback.

For follow-up to be effective, you must give your employees feedback. You need to let them know how they're doing. Don't force them to guess. They need your feedback to know what to do differently and how to improve. Without it, they'll just continue down the same path. It's your responsibility to tell them whether they're on the *right* path. It's difficult to work effectively toward goals when you don't know how you're doing. Research shows that job performance usually suffers when people don't get feedback. Uncertainty detracts from people's ability to focus on the goals. So make sure you give your employees feedback as they work on delegated tasks. Don't leave them wondering how they're doing.

*"The great thing in this world is not so much where we are, but in what direction we are moving."*

*— Oliver Wendell Holmes*

198

## EXERCISE

Consider a delegated task you're currently working on. Think about discussions you've had with your manager about the task since he or she first delegated it, then answer the following questions.

- What is the task? _____
_____

|  | YES | NO |
|---|---|---|
| Did your manager hold a delegation conference with you? | ___ | ___ |
| Did he or she discuss a follow-up plan during the delegation conference? | ___ | ___ |
| Did the plan specify how your manager would monitor your progress on the task? | ___ | ___ |
| Did your manager discuss giving you feedback while you work on the task? | ___ | ___ |
| Are you getting feedback from your manager as you progress toward your goals? | ___ | ___ |
| If so, has the feedback helped you achieve your objectives? | ___ | ___ |

If you answered "yes" to all these questions, your manager is a conscientious delegator who recognizes the importance of feedback. Learn from your experience and make sure you give feedback to your employees. If you answered "no" to many of the questions, talk with your manager and emphasize the importance of feedback to you.

## Feedback Types

There are two basic types of feedback.

1.  Feedback can encourage and reinforce your employee when the delegated task is going well.

2.  Feedback can modify or correct your employee's approach when problems develop or when you're concerned about successful completion of the task.

The first type of feedback is straightforward and is often neglected because some managers see no need for it. You may be tempted not to give feedback when a delegated task is going well. Why bother to compliment your employee if progress is apparent and you don't see any problems? You can praise the person when the task is finished, right? Wrong.

Remember the research results — job performance usually suffers when people don't get feedback. Show your interest in the project. If progress is apparent, *tell* your employees that. Commend them for what's been accomplished already. Express your appreciation for their efforts, their organizational skills and their creativity. It takes so little time to give a few words of praise and encouragement, yet the payback can be great.

If the project *is* going well, you want it to *continue* to go well. Tell your employees you're impressed with their approach and pleased with their progress. Mention you think they've chosen the right path to the goals. Don't neglect feedback just because a delegated task is on track and on schedule. Show your employees you know how to praise as well as criticize. This will strengthen your relationship with them and make it easier for you to interact with them on more difficult subjects in the future. It's always appropriate to show appreciation to your employees for good work, even if the task isn't finished yet.

> *"There are two basic types of feedback:*
>
> *1) To encourage and reinforce;*
>
> *2) To modify or correct."*

## Criticism in Delegation

The second type of feedback that modifies or corrects your employee's approach usually involves criticism. Sometimes as you monitor progress of a delegated task, you find it's *not* going well. Maybe your employee has chosen an approach you know won't work, or maybe he's not using the required resources. Or maybe he's lost sight of the goals. Whatever the reason, you recognize corrective action is needed or your employee is likely to fail and not complete the task successfully. You need to give timely feedback to get the task back on track, and the feedback probably must include criticism.

If you're like most people, the mere mention of the word criticism makes you squirm. Let's be honest, no one likes to be criticized. The word usually reminds us of unpleasant experiences. It definitely has negative implications. Receiving criticism is painful, and it's not much fun to give it either. But to become a great delegator, you must learn to criticize your people, because criticism is an essential element of feedback. And to be a great manager, you must learn to accept and even seek criticism, because it can help you improve and develop.

Originally, "to criticize" meant "to judge accordingly." The word had no inherent negative meaning. However, today it almost always implies something negative. When we think of criticism, we seldom react positively. If the level of criticism aimed at us exceeds a certain threshold, we get defensive and may completely tune out the person doing the criticizing. Criticism attacks our self-esteem, and that hurts. It can also cause severe stress and affect morale and job performance. Unless it's given skillfully, criticism can devastate us. But you *can* make criticism a powerful force for positive change and improvement. As a manager, you need to develop the skill to give constructive criticism. By using it properly, you can help your people complete delegated tasks successfully. And it's a skill you also need for your other responsibilities as a manager. When you discuss performance with your employees, the way you criticize them affects their attitude toward changing their behavior. Skillful use of constructive criticism shows you want to help them improve. Destructive criticism usually makes them defensive and resistant to change.

*"To escape criticism — do nothing, say nothing, be nothing."*

*— Elbert Hubbard*

## EXERCISE

Recall the last time your manager criticized you. Think about your reaction.

- How did you feel?

- What did you say?

- Do you think the criticism was justified?

- Did you find it difficult to accept?

- Did it cause you to modify your behavior in any way?

Giving and taking criticism is tough for all of us. Yet you must learn to use criticism constructively to grow in your job and help your employees develop in theirs. To rise above the negative aspects of criticism, you need to develop a conviction that criticism is necessary for improvement to happen. Even though it creates discomfort in you and others, you must learn to use criticism as a means to improve your people and yourself. In the following pages we'll discuss how to do that.

## Types of Criticism

Let's consider the characteristics of constructive and destructive criticism. Destructive criticism is meant to punish, manipulate or embarrass. Its effect is almost always negative. Constructive criticism is supportive and encouraging; improvement is its primary goal.

The language you use when you criticize often shows whether your criticism is constructive or destructive. Let's look at some examples.

## EXAMPLE #1

You've delegated to Bill the task of writing three reports for the division director. In the delegation conference you covered very carefully what topics he should include in the reports. As part of your follow-up, you asked Bill to meet with you when he finishes the first report. You've read the first one, and Bill missed the mark. Consider these two approaches to criticism:

a) "You've done it again, Bill. You *never* listen when I tell you what to do. I counted on you, and you let me down. You should rewrite this report."

b) "Before you begin working on the second report, Bill, let's discuss what you might include to strengthen it. And I think the first one would be more effective if you add a section on equipment maintenance when you revise it."

Note in the first response that you accuse Bill and try to make him feel guilty. He's sure to become resentful and won't welcome your suggestions. The result will likely be a poorly rewritten first report, as well as other reports too. In the second response you've tried to be helpful and supportive. You focus on *improving* the reports, not on accusing him of failure. He'll likely appreciate your suggestions and act on them.

> "It is a very delicate job to forgive a man, without lowering him in his own estimation, and yours too."
>
> — *Josh Billings*

Example

## Example

## EXAMPLE #2

You've asked Helen to design the equipment layout for the new plant. As part of follow-up, you've asked her to sketch her preliminary plan and review it with you. You see from the sketch that her plan does not allow enough space to move parts to and from the machines.

Consider these two approaches:

a)  "Look what you've done, Helen. You failed to consider the space necessary to move the parts to and from the machines. You obviously didn't think very carefully when you designed this. Now try to do it right!"

b)  "Basically, I like the layout of the machines you propose, Helen. You might want to check the dimensions of the aisles again to be sure you can get parts to the machines without any problems."

In the first response you've used language that will put Helen on the defensive. Phrases like "Look what you've done," "You've failed ... " and "You didn't think ... " are destructive. In the second response you show you like her basic design but you suggest in a non-threatening way that she check the dimensions again. You offer constructive criticism to help her improve her design.

Your language and tone of voice strongly affect how your employee reacts to your criticism. You should avoid accusations, anger and sarcasm. They are elements of destructive criticism and will only make the situation worse.

*Destructive* criticism usually involves phrases like:

- You always ...
- You should ...
- You never ...
- You ought ...
- You let me down ...
- You disappoint me ...
- You don't really care ...
- Look at what you've done ...
- You failed to ...

Or you may say destructive things like:

- I don't want to hear your excuses ...
- This shows you don't care ...
- After all I've done for you ...

When offering *constructive* criticism, use phrases like:

- I know this is difficult for you, so let's try to ...
- Let's consider how we can improve this ...
- I'd prefer if you ...
- I like your approach and have a question about ...
- What would you suggest we do about ...
- Let's work together to make this ...
- I know we can strengthen this by ...

Note the cooperative, supportive tone of these phrases. You show you want to help, not blame. Your intent is to improve the situation, not punish the person. With such constructive comments you set the stage for improvement. And that should be the purpose of criticism.

## Attitude Toward Criticism

Although language and tone of voice are important in criticism, you can't ignore attitude. In fact, your attitude determines what language and tone of voice you use. As we discussed earlier, most of us automatically think of criticism as something negative. If that's our attitude, it will show in how we give and take criticism. If you view criticism as negative, you'll react negatively when criticized. You'll also trigger negative reactions in your employees when you criticize them. You must change your attitude about criticism and view it as positive. Only then can you use it as a force for positive change and improvement. Both the giver and the receiver of criticism must view it as positive or the potential benefits of constructive criticism will be lost.

*"On the occasion of every accident that befalls you, remember to turn to yourself and inquire what power you have for turning it to use."*

*— Epictetus*

> *"As a delegator, your attitude toward criticism is important ... If you want to be a successful delegator, you must develop a positive attitude toward criticism and learn to use it effectively."*

Consider the importance of attitude in these two possible reactions by someone who has just been criticized.

a) "She's always finding fault with my work. She's never satisfied and always stresses my mistakes."

b) "She's made some valuable suggestions. My report will be better if I listen to her."

In the first case, the person is upset and defensive. He views all criticism as negative, so his reaction is predictable. He focuses on his resentment toward the criticizer, instead of improving his performance. In the second case, the employee recognizes the value of criticism and uses it to improve his report.

Your attitude toward criticism is the key to how well you give and take criticism. If you're mired in a negative attitude, you'll never learn how to use criticism to help yourself grow. You'll always try to avoid it because it causes only pain. You'll communicate your negative attitude to your people, and you'll never learn to use criticism to help them develop. By hurdling this negative attitude, you can open up tremendous possibilities for yourself and your people. You'll recognize that criticism is a powerful force for change and growth. You can learn from it, and you can help others by using it skillfully. But you *must* develop a positive attitude toward it. That's the key.

As a delegator, your attitude toward criticism is important. When you delegate a task, you're responsible for following up on it. That follow-up will require feedback. You'll probably have to criticize your employee in a constructive way so he or she can complete the task successfully. If your attitude toward criticism is negative, you'll transmit that attitude to your employee. At a time when the person needs support and encouragement to do a good job, you'll discourage him or her through negative, destructive criticism. If you want to be a successful delegator, you *must* develop a positive attitude toward criticism and learn to use it effectively.

## EXERCISE

Recall the last time you gave feedback to one of your employees working on a delegated task. Think about the feedback and the criticism you offered, then answer the following questions.

- When you offered the feedback, was it to reinforce what your employee was doing or did you need to modify or correct the employee's approach?

  _____

  _____

- If you had to modify or correct the approach, you had to *criticize* your employee. When you recall the words you used, would you say you gave your employee *constructive* or *destructive* criticism?

  _____

- What phrases did you use?

  _____

  _____

  _____

  _____

- How did your employee react to your criticism?

  _____

  _____

  _____

  _____

## EXERCISE (Continued)

- How would you describe his or her attitude toward criticism?

  _____

  _____

  _____

  _____

- At the time you offered the feedback, what was *your* attitude toward criticism? Did you view it as negative or something positive that could lead to change and growth?

  _____

  _____

  _____

  _____

## The Benefits of Criticism

You can use criticism to constantly remind your people of their mistakes and failures, or you can use it to help them develop and improve. You can give destructive criticism or you can give constructive criticism. It's your choice. The effective manager and delegator chooses the latter. But why? What are the advantages and benefits of constructive criticism?

UCLA psychologist Hendrie Weisinger has done extensive research on criticism. In his book, *The Critical Edge*, he gives five reasons why "productive criticism" is invaluable to individual and organizational success. He says productive or constructive criticism:

- Provides feedback that enhances job results
- Leads to ongoing personal and professional development
- Reduces stress and creates psychological security
- Helps improve interpersonal relationships
- Helps develop the ideal organizational climate

(From *The Critical Edge: How to Criticize Up and Down Your Organization and Make It Pay Off*, Hendrie Weisinger. Copyright 1989, Hendrie Weisinger, Ph.D., by permission of Little, Brown & Co.)

Let's see how these points relate to criticism in delegation. Remember, criticism is an element of feedback, and you should give your employees feedback as you follow up on delegated tasks.

**Constructive criticism provides feedback that enhances job results.** This may be the strongest link between productive criticism and delegation. When you give feedback to your employee working on a delegated task, you want to help him or her complete the task successfully. You want to enhance the job results. By giving constructive criticism in feedback, you help your employee assess progress on the project. You set the stage for improvement. With constructive criticism, your employee knows what action to take to get back on track. Your criticism increases the likelihood the person will complete the task successfully.

**Constructive criticism leads to ongoing personal and professional development.** One of the primary purposes of delegation is to help your people develop. Delegation spurs them to learn, grow and take on new responsibility. When you delegate, you create a situation that *should* lead to development for your employees. But it's not automatic. It depends on your behavior as the delegator. You must offer feedback for your employees to reap the full benefits of

> *" ... Criticism is an element of feedback."*

209

delegation. And that usually involves giving criticism. Constructive criticism shows your employees that you care about them and want to help them grow.

**Constructive criticism reduces stress and creates psychological security.** If you delegate a task and neglect feedback, your employee will probably feel uneasy. He won't be sure how well the task is going or what to do to improve. Lack of feedback in such situations can be very stressful. In fact, lack of feedback is a major cause of job-related stress. As a manager, you can relieve that stress by following up when you delegate. Give your employees constructive criticism. Let them know how the task is progressing and suggest ways they can improve. Let them know you want to help. Today's workplace creates enough stress. Do what you can to reduce it. Your employees will be more productive, and you'll be a better manager.

**Constructive criticism helps improve interpersonal relationships.** When you offer constructive criticism to your employees as they work on delegated tasks, you send a message that you're interested in their success, growth and development. You show you don't believe in delegating a task and then walking away. You show you care. That helps build your relationship with your employees. Constructive criticism says, "I want to help, and here are ways you can improve." Such an approach is almost sure to strengthen relationships with your people.

**Constructive criticism helps develop the ideal organizational climate.** If you give your employees feedback and constructive criticism *every time* you delegate, you create an environment where criticism is accepted and recognized as a force for positive change. Others who work with you will throw out their negative opinion of criticism and realize its benefits. Where constructive criticism is the norm in an organization, people are free to criticize one another without hard feelings. Everyone realizes that improvement of the individuals and the entire organization is the goal. People don't have to be defensive, because criticism is constructive. The climate of the entire organization improves, and morale gets a real boost.

As a manager, you can influence how your organization uses and perceives criticism. Your attitude and behavior communicate more to your people than you may realize. Never underestimate your ability to influence your organization positively *or* negatively. How you handle both giving and receiving feedback and criticism is a major factor that determines the impact you have. Constructive criticism is powerful and can strengthen your people and your company. But don't forget, destructive criticism is powerful too. You can do tremendous damage when you use it. Your employees may become demotivated, resentful or share their newly acquired poor attitude with co-workers by gossiping or grousing. And if you're insensitive, you may not even realize the pain you've caused.

Whenever a situation requires that you criticize your people, think about what you're doing. Don't hurl accusations because you're determined to "correct" the situation. With that approach, you'll just make things worse. Criticize your people constructively. Help them get back on track and improve. Use your experience to help them. Guide them in the right direction and help them avoid approaches you *know* will fail. Show them you care about them as people and as employees. You'll be amazed at what you can accomplish when you learn to use feedback and criticism skillfully. You'll see results in your people and in your organization. Your people will welcome criticism because they'll realize it can help them improve. Your organization will be stronger because your people will be determined to improve. And your effectiveness as a manager will increase.

*"You'll be amazed at what you can accomplish when you learn to use feedback and criticism skillfully."*

**Case Study**

Marie is a competent, highly regarded employee. Glenn is her manager who recognizes her capability and tries to develop her skills by delegating important tasks to her. She seems to be progressing well, so he decides to delegate a major research project to her. He thinks she'll take five months to complete it. If she does well on this job, he'll promote her when it's finished.

Three months have passed since Marie started the major research project. She asks to meet with Glenn.

"This is very difficult for me, Glenn, but I'm giving two weeks' notice. I've accepted a job with Norton Company, and I start there June 1."

Glenn's jaw drops. He can't believe what he's just heard. His best employee's leaving! But why? Before he can ask, Marie continues.

"You've delegated several challenging tasks to me, and I appreciate that. But you don't follow up. You don't give me any feedback. I don't know where I stand. I don't know whether you think my work is great or you just tolerate it. I send you reports and keep you advised, but nothing comes back. I'm in a fog of uncertainty, and I just can't work that way. I need constructive criticism to know how to improve. I need the benefit of your knowledge and experience. I had hoped to have a long career here, but I can't take the stress. I have to make a change. Sorry."

**Analysis**

Glenn truly considered Marie to be an outstanding employee. Unfortunately, he never told her that. He failed to give her feedback on how she was doing or how she could improve. He assumed she knew. She was so unhappy she felt she had to change jobs to escape the stress. Clearly, Glenn was not sensitive to her needs for feedback. That lack of sensitivity cost the company an outstanding employee.

Never assume your employees don't need feedback or criticism. They do. They may not ask for it, but as the manager, you're responsible for providing it. Learn to give it skillfully.

**Questions**

- If you were Glenn, what would you have done differently?

  _____

  _____

- How do you think Marie would have responded to constructive criticism?

  _____

  _____

- What kind of feedback would have reduced her stress?

  _____

  _____

## Feedback, Criticism and Continuous Improvement

The concepts of feedback, criticism and continuous improvement are closely related, and it's useful to explore those relationships. Recall the meaning of *kaizen* — ongoing improvement involving everyone. The kaizen philosophy says your entire way of life deserves to be continuously improved. Don't be satisfied with the way things are, make them better! Such an approach *requires* continuous feedback and criticism so you can make changes that lead to improvement. Without feedback, you don't know what to do to improve. Without constructive criticism, you don't know what changes to make.

Earlier we discussed the value of continuous improvement as a workplace strategy. Even if your company does not have a formal program, you can use the general philosophy within your group or section. As a manager, you have influence. Try to motivate your people to adopt continuous improvement as a way of life. Remember our saying:

> **"If it ain't broke, fix it anyway and make it better."**

With that philosophy in place, feedback and criticism are natural and expected. Your people realize that feedback and criticism are keys to improvement for themselves and for the organization. Instead of avoiding criticism, they'll seek it because they realize how it leads to improvement. Once you've established the mind-set in your people that criticism is good and necessary for growth and improvement, you can make great progress.

It's exciting to work with a group that believes in continuous improvement and knows constructive criticism is vital to the process. The group works toward a common goal — improvement of the organization and its practices, policies and procedures. Everything is fair game because everything can be improved. Most important of all, the employees work to improve themselves. A climate develops that allows and encourages the free flow of critical information. Everyone realizes criticism is offered for the good of the group, so all the employees become less defensive. They cooperate, and the results are impressive.

*"Your people realize that feedback and criticism are keys to improvement."*

214

## The Manager's Role

As a manager, you set the tone for your group. How you take criticism and how you use it greatly affect your people. If you hang on to the traditional belief that criticism is negative and something to avoid, your people will too. You have to change that belief to make progress. If you can't convince yourself of criticism's positive potential, you probably won't convince anyone else. But you *must* convince yourself, because developing a healthy attitude toward criticism is necessary for you to be an effective manager. You *need* a healthy attitude toward criticism because you must learn how to take it to improve yourself. And you must *believe* in criticism as a powerful force for change so you can help your employees improve. So after you've convinced yourself of the positive role of criticism, educate and convince your people.

> *"He that would govern others, first should be the master of himself."*
>
> — *Philip Massinger*

215

## EXERCISE

Gauge your attitude toward criticism by reviewing a delegation example. Recall a task you delegated recently, preferably one that involved more than simple, noncritical feedback from you. Then answer the following questions.

- What was the task?

_____

|  | YES | NO |
|---|---|---|
| • Did you hold a delegation conference when you assigned it? | —— | —— |
| • Did you agree on a feedback plan with your employee? | —— | —— |
| • Did you criticize your employee's progress while giving feedback? | —— | —— |
| • Would you describe your criticism as *constructive*? (Be honest!) | —— | —— |
| • Did you point out ways your employee could improve? | —— | —— |
| • Did you suggest approaches that would make success more likely? | —— | —— |
| • Did you stress your desire to help your employee succeed with the task? | —— | —— |

If you answered "yes" to most of the questions, you probably recognize the importance of feedback that includes constructive criticism. But let's explore a little further.

## EXERCISE (Continued)

- If you described your criticism as "constructive," what characteristics made you classify it that way?

  _____

  _____

  _____

- How did your employee react to your criticism?

  _____

  _____

  _____

- If you said your criticism was "destructive," what did you say or do to make it so?

  _____

  _____

  _____

- What was your employee's reaction?

  _____

  _____

  _____

- What will you do differently next time you offer criticism?

  _____

  _____

  _____

## Keys to Constructive Criticism

Let's assume you're now convinced criticism doesn't have to be negative. What can you do to improve your ability to criticize in a constructive way?

As mentioned earlier, UCLA psychologist Hendrie Weisinger has done extensive research on criticism. From his studies he's found the following seven factors that set the stage for productive criticism.

1. Productive criticism is strategic.

2. Productive criticism protects self-esteem.

3. Productive criticism is timing-oriented.

4. Productive criticism is improvement-oriented.

5. Productive criticism is interactive.

6. Productive criticism is flexible.

7. Productive criticism communicates the helping spirit.

(From *The Critical Edge: How to Criticize Up and Down Your Organization and Make It Pay Off,* Hendrie Weisinger. Copyright 1989, Hendrie Weisinger, Ph.D., by permission of Little Brown & Co.)

How can we relate these factors to criticism in delegation?

1. **Be strategic.** The key to being strategic in your criticism is to plan ahead. Think about what to say before you say it. Don't spout off, especially if you're angry. Decide what you want to accomplish, organize your thoughts and choose your words carefully. You may even want to write down what you plan to say. Review your words, and be sure they say what you mean.

   If you've just learned that Greg annoyed an important customer while giving that presentation you delegated to him and you see him walking toward you, don't give your feedback now! You need time to cool off and think about what to say. You want to help him, not demoralize him. Your goal is to offer constructive criticism, and that's hard to do when you're angry. So plan before you criticize.

> *"Before beginning, prepare carefully."*
>
> *— Cicero*

2.  **Protect self-esteem.** Remember, self-esteem is a fragile thing that's precious to every person. It's so easy to hurt people with criticism, so easy to attack their self-esteem. And it's so destructive. Give criticism in a way that protects self-esteem. Avoid accusations. Watch your language. Don't attack or accuse the person, rather offer suggestions about the task.

    If Tim is late with the report you asked him to write, don't launch into him with "Late again" or "Can't you ever be on time?" Instead try, "Do you need typing assistance to finish your project?" or "What information do you still need to finish the report?" Reconfirm your need for the report, but be supportive.

3.  **Be timing-oriented.** Always consider the time, place and circumstances for giving criticism. Decide what's the best combination of these to ensure your employee will be most receptive. Usually a one-on-one discussion between you and your employee is best, but there may be exceptions. For example, if your group has advanced to the point that criticism is open and welcome, you may give criticism successfully in a group meeting. Then the entire group can offer support. You must choose the time and place, keeping the individual and circumstances in mind.

    For example, Ted's hit a roadblock in the research project you've delegated to him and is ready to give up. You think a brainstorming session with other group members would give him fresh ideas and get him moving again. Since your group is cohesive and supportive, you use the group meeting to mention Ted's problem and seek suggestions from the group.

4.  **Be improvement-oriented.** Always focus on the future when giving criticism. Don't stress past mistakes. Talk about how to do things better and how to improve. Emphasizing mistakes puts your employee on the defensive and is counterproductive. Discussing ways to improve shows you want to help and conditions your employee to accept your criticism and then move forward. You'll find this approach to be natural if your organization believes in continuous improvement.

> *"One man finds pleasure in improving his land, another his horses. My pleasure lies in seeing that I myself grow better day by day."*
>
> *— Socrates*

219

Say you've asked George to prepare the financial summary this month to give him experience. He used an outdated computer program, and his results are incorrect. Don't blast him with "That was dumb!" or "We can't use this worthless data." Instead, look to the future and show your support. Say "You'll probably find the new program easier to use next time" or "You can improve the presentation of your data by using the new program."

5. **Be interactive.** Giving negative criticism tends to be a one-way process. You run through a litany of your employee's mistakes while he or she sits there getting more upset. As you keep talking, your employee may tune you out. Positive results probably won't emerge from such a session. You must involve the other person. You must give criticism in an interactive way to get the benefits of it. Bring your employee into the conversation. You want to participate in a dialogue, not give a lecture.

For example, you asked Marlene to organize the material you must take on your trip. You arrive at your destination, and several important slides are missing. You have to rewrite your talk to work around those missing slides. When you get back to the office, don't recite all her faults: "You're disorganized, careless, sloppy and unable to plan." Instead, try to involve her in a discussion of how to improve her procedures. Try saying, "Marlene, can you think of any better procedures we can use to organize our slides? We've got so many now that we need a better way." Or "I wonder if I've neglected to tell you what I need for these trips. Can you tell me what additional information would make the job easier for you?"

6. **Be flexible.** Destructive criticizers tend to be rigid thinkers. They know what *they* want to say, and their goal is to get it said. You should tell the employee what his mistakes are and be done with it. Destructive criticizers aren't interested in an exchange of ideas. They've got their agendas and don't want to vary from them. However, when you criticize, as in most things you do as a manager, be flexible. Let your employee tell you how he feels. Ask for his

*"When giving criticism, you want to participate in a dialogue, not give a lecture."*

ideas. Encourage suggestions. Adjust your
conversation as you get feedback. If you see your
employee getting defensive, change your approach.
Always be flexible. Plan your criticism ahead of time,
but be prepared to modify your plan if the situation
requires it.

Suppose you asked Teresa to take some customers
on a plant tour and demonstrate operation of the
new packaging machine. The demonstration was a
disaster. You're meeting with her to discuss what
went wrong. Although you planned your criticism
carefully, you see that your remarks are upsetting
her. Change your approach. Involve her more in the
discussion. Ask her what you can do to help her. Ask
her what could be done to improve tours for
customers. If your original approach isn't working,
try a different one. And if that doesn't work, try a
third one. Be flexible.

7. **Communicate the helping spirit.** To criticize
   constructively, you must communicate the helping
   spirit to your employees. You must let them know:

   - You care about them
   - You're confident they can improve
   - You're committed to helping them

Tell them and show them by your actions. Stand by
them when they have troubles. Don't focus on their
mistakes, but stress ways to improve. Praise them for
their accomplishments. Demonstrate your confidence
in them by delegating additional tasks. Show them
you're committed to help by offering suggestions. Let
this spirit guide all interactions with your employees,
not just those where you delegate tasks or give
criticism.

By communicating the helping spirit, you'll
strengthen relationships with your people. Their
confidence and trust in you will increase, and they'll
be more receptive to your suggestions for
improvement. Remember, as the manager, you have
influence and should set the tone for your group.

*"Don't focus on mistakes — stress ways to improve."*

221

> *"It's what you learn after you know it all that counts."*
>
> *— John Wooden*

Communicate the helping spirit to your entire group. It will create an environment where mutual support and help are the norm.

## Summary

Feedback and criticism are essential to the delegation process. Without them the process isn't complete. Remember that your people *need* feedback and criticism to know how to improve. It's your responsibility to provide them. Abandon the conventional wisdom that criticism is negative and destructive. Give constructive criticism and show your people you want to help them improve. Communicate the helping spirit. Your organization will be more effective, and you'll keep growing as a manager.

## QUESTIONS FOR PERSONAL DEVELOPMENT

1.    What is the major emphasis of this chapter?

2.    What do you feel are the most important things you learned from this chapter?

   1)

   2)

   3)

3. How can you apply what you learned to your current job?

   1)

   2)

   3)

4. What objectives will you set for improvement? By when (date)?

   **Objective:**                **By When?**

   1)

   2)

   3)

5. Who can help you most in applying what you learned in this chapter?

6. What are the major roadblocks that might hinder your progress in applying what you learned in this chapter?

**Roadblock:**                       **Why?**

1)

2)

3)

7. How will you communicate the most important points in this chapter to others in your organization?

8. What preparation is necessary to introduce better delegation?

9. What changes do you expect to make that will better motivate your team?

**Change:**                       **By when?**

1)

2)

3)

10. How will you monitor your progress to assure that performance has improved or productivity has increased? (reports, meetings, etc.)

11. What work-related problems concern you most in evaluating how you will benefit from this chapter?

12. What changes do you expect to see in yourself one year from now as a result of what you learned in this chapter?

# **E** *PILOGUE*

In the movie *Dead Poets Society,* Robin Williams plays a literature teacher at a boys' prep school in New England. He's unconventional, but inspires his students. He pushes them to reach out and experience the world around them. "*Carpe diem!*" he tells them, which translates literally as "Seize the day!" He urges them to take advantage of opportunity whenever it presents itself, because that opportunity may never come again.

That's a good philosophy for you as a manager, too. Take advantage of your opportunities. Use them to improve your people, your organization and yourself. Seize opportunities to delegate. Delegation is a powerful way to develop your employees and increase your value to the organization. Use it skillfully.

Yes, you should seize opportunities that come along. But better yet, create them yourself. Be proactive. Always look for ways to improve your people and yourself. Your contributions and those of your employees will grow. The entire organization will benefit. And you'll find tremendous satisfaction.

*Carpe diem!*

> *"The reason a lot of people do not recognize opportunity is because it usually goes around wearing overalls looking like hard work."*
>
> *— Thomas Alva Edison*

> *"A wise man will make more opportunity than he finds."*
>
> *— Francis Bacon*

227

# $I$ NDEX

# C

# D

## E

## F

## G

## H

## I

## J

## K

## L

# M

manager's expectations,　140
Massinger, Philip,　215
McGowan, William G.,　19

# N

Newton, Howard W.,　165
Nietzsche, Friedrich,　160

# O

occupational hobbies,　38, 54

# P

Patton, George S.,　158
Perot, H. Ross,　40
personnel matters,　61
Piatt, Donn,　20
policy-making,　62
Prochnow, Herbert V.,　190
*Pygmalion,*　140
"Pygmalion-in-Management Effect,"　140

# R

Roberts, Edgar F.,　41
Rodman, David M.,　192
Rogers, J.R.,　8
Rogers, Will,　54
Roosevelt, Theodore,　178
Rosenberger, Homer T.,　7

# Other Training Resources Available From National Press Publications

## Desktop Handbooks

**National Press Publications Desktop Handbooks** take the essentials of an important subject and distill them into a focused, concise handbook that's short (no more than 120 pages), easy to use and convenient. Their durable spiral binding allows them to lie flat on your desktop and the high quality manufacture means they'll stay with you all the way to the boardroom. The books in this series have sold more than a million copies for one simple reason — because people recognize outstanding quality and value when they see it. Each book is a gold mine of instant information you'll turn to again and again. We guarantee it!

### The Leadership Series

| Qty | Item # | Title | U.S. | Can. | Total |
|-----|--------|-------|------|------|-------|
| | 410 | The Supervisor's Handbook, Revised and Expanded | $12.95 | $14.95 | |
| | 418 | Total Quality Management | $12.95 | $14.95 | |
| | 459 | Techniques of Successful Delegation | $12.95 | $14.95 | |
| | 463 | Powerful Leadership Skills for Women | $12.95 | $14.95 | |
| | 469 | Peak Performance | $12.95 | $14.95 | |
| | 494 | Team-Building | $12.95 | $14.95 | |
| | 495 | How to Manage Conflict | $12.95 | $14.95 | |

### The Communication Series

| Qty | Item # | Title | U.S. | Can. | Total |
|-----|--------|-------|------|------|-------|
| | 413 | Dynamic Communication Skills for Women | $12.95 | $14.95 | |
| | 414 | The Write Stuff: *A Style Manual for Effective Business Writing* | $12.95 | $14.95 | |
| | 417 | Listen Up: *Hear What's Really Being Said* | $12.95 | $14.95 | |
| | 442 | Assertiveness: *Get What You Want Without Being Pushy* | $12.95 | $14.95 | |
| | 460 | Techniques to Improve Your Writing Skills | $12.95 | $14.95 | |
| | 461 | Powerful Presentation Skills | $12.95 | $14.95 | |
| | 482 | Techniques of Effective Telephone Communication | $12.95 | $14.95 | |
| | 485 | Personal Negotiating Skills | $12.95 | $14.95 | |
| | 488 | Customer Service: *The Key to Winning Lifetime Customers* | $12.95 | $14.95 | |
| | 498 | How to Manage Your Boss | $12.95 | $14.95 | |

### The Productivity Series

| Qty | Item # | Title | U.S. | Can. | Total |
|-----|--------|-------|------|------|-------|
| | 411 | Getting Things Done: *An Achievers Guide to Time Management* | $12.95 | $14.95 | |
| | 443 | A New Attitude | $12.95 | $14.95 | |
| | 468 | Understanding the Bottom Line: *Finance for the Non-Financial Manager* | $12.95 | $14.95 | |
| | 489 | Doing Business Over the Phone: *Telemarketing for the the 90's* | $12.95 | $14.95 | |
| | 496 | Motivation & Goal-Setting: *The Keys to Achieving Success* | $12.95 | $14.95 | |

# Desktop Handbooks Continued

## The Lifestyle Series

| Qty | Item # | Title | U.S. | Can. | Total |
|---|---|---|---|---|---|
| | 415 | Balancing Career & Family: *Overcoming the Superwoman Syndrome* | $12.95 | $14.95 | |
| | 416 | Real Men Don't Vacuum | $12.95 | $14.95 | |
| | 464 | Self-Esteem: *The Power to Be Your Best* | $12.95 | $14.95 | |
| | 484 | The Stress Management Handbook | $12.95 | $14.95 | |
| | 486 | Parenting: *Ward & June Don't Live Here Anymore* | $12.95 | $14.95 | |
| | 487 | How to Get the Job You Want | $12.95 | $14.95 | |

## Business User's Manuals

| Qty | Item # | Title | U.S. | Can. | Total |
|---|---|---|---|---|---|
| | 436 | Delegate — Multiply Your Impact | $24.95 | $28.95 | |
| | 447 | To Meet or Not to Meet: *How to Plan and Conduct Effective Meetings* | $24.95 | $28.95 | |
| | 449 | Business Letters for Busy People | $24.95 | $28.95 | |
| | 451 | Think Like a Manager | $24.95 | $28.95 | |
| | 452 | The Memory System | $24.95 | $28.95 | |
| | 453 | Prioritize ... Organize ... *The Art of Getting It Done* | $24.95 | $28.95 | |
| | 454 | Total Quality Management | $24.95 | $28.95 | |

### Sales Tax

All purchases subject to applicable sales tax. Questions? Call **1-800-258-7248**

| | |
|---|---|
| Subtotal | |
| Sales Tax (see note) | |
| Shipping and Handling ($1 one item; 50¢ each additional) | |
| Total | |

Name _____ Title_____

Organization _____

Address _____ City _____

State/Province _____ ZIP/Postal Code _____

## Method of Payment

❏ Enclosed is my check or money order payable to National Seminars
❏ Please charge to: ❏ MasterCard ❏ Visa ❏ American Express

Signature _____ Exp. Date _____

Card Number_____

*Complete and send entire page by mail to:*

**IN U.S.A.**
**National Press Publications**
A Division of Rockhurst College
Continuing Education Center
6901 W. 63rd Street • P.O. Box 2949
• Shawnee Mission, KS 66201-1349

**IN CANADA**
**National Press Publications**
A Division of Rockhurst College
Continuing Education Center
1243 Islington Ave., Suite 900
Toronto, Ontario M8X 1Y9

*Or call TOLL-FREE 1-800-258-7248 or FAX (913) 432-0824*
VIP #705-08436-092